VISIONS FROM THE HEART

VISIONS FROM THE HEART

JENNIFER JAMES, PH.D.

NEWMARKET PRESS
New York

93 94 95   10 9 8 7 6 5 4 3 2 1

Library of Congress Cataloging-in-Publication Data

James, Jennifer, 1943-
Visions from the Heart/Jennifer James
p. cm.
ISBN: 1-55704-141-5
1. Visions (spiritual). 2. Personal growth (psychology).
3. Conduct of life. I. Title.
1991   91-058783 CIP

Manufactured in the United States of America

First Newmarket Edition

Book cover and interior design by Tania Garcia
Interior illustrations by Ray Pelley

Quantity Purchases
Companies, professional groups, clubs, and other organizations may qualify for special terms when ordering quantities of this title. For information, contact the Special Sales Department, Newmarket Press, 18 East 48th Street, New York, N.Y. 10017. Phone (212) 832-3575.

Author Speaking Engagements
For information regarding speaking engagements by Jennifer James, please contact the author directly at P.O. Box 337, Seahurst, Washington 98062.

DEDICATION

My life has drawn its greatest strength and love from the earth. The light, color, smell, pulse, sound, and feel of being raised on a farm is always with me. I thought I was not as fortunate as some who drew their love, early in life, from others.

Yet I, too, am blessed. I found the Northwest on my own, I found Seattle. I found love. This book is for the earth and the life that surrounds us.

There is no love that rewards more consistently than the love one has for the world.

CONTENTS

ILLUSTRATIONS

ACKNOWLEDGMENTS

A book, even a little book, is a contribution of many hands and minds working together.

Alberta Stone, Diana Stice, and Charlotte Bottoms have been volunteers with the Community Service Committee for many years. They answer letters, make telephone calls, and provide information, referrals, and love just because they care. Each contributed an essay to this book, although they are reluctant to appear in print. They are my friends, godmothers to me in many ways. They were sent to heal the past, and they have done so. Bertie, Diana, and Charlotte edited, arranged, designed, typed, and joked until this manuscript came together.

Alice Godfrey made all the complex arrangements for assembling and publishing this book. She did it all, as usual, with her uncommon energy, good humor, and competence.

Walli Stemmer is my executive assistant. She kept the office and me together, as always, with her warmth, intelligence, intensity, and hard work.

Elizabeth Miller and Judy Ziegler helped to edit and organize this material into book form. Debby Boyer, Ph.D., a friend and colleague, helped me with the research but is in no way responsible for how I have used it.

Ray Pelley is a Seattle artist who sees the world in unique and visionary ways. His work also appeared in the original edition of *Windows*. He created all of the interior illustrations.

Bronwen Press, which originally issued this volume in a slightly different format, is our own way of publishing books quietly. Bronwen is Welsh for "strong friend" or "beautiful brow." It is my middle name.

Jennifer James
Seattle, April 1993

BEGINNING THE JOURNEY

Throughout time, individuals with heart and passion have sought greater power, intimate connections with the universe, and a sense of their own destiny. The intensity of this quest either increases with age, as life experience enhances trust of our own stirrings, or wanes as we stop believing that all things are possible. Visionaries are always drawn down the path to deeper understanding. Joseph Campbell says, "They hear the call."

Visionaries have an ability to see or feel beyond the present, to imagine, to create, and to feel safe with what is to come or what has been. A vision is a thought or feeling that can come to any one of the senses at any time. Visions can be a combination of intuition, dreams, hopes, values, and beliefs. We can learn through all aspects of our intelligence and our awareness. It is even possible to smell knowledge.

When I was struggling with my own path, the journey took me deep into the earliest time of my life and a very powerful smell—the smell of workingmen, of a man who worked in the coal mines. The smell was of my father. I did not understand, until that moment in my forties, why I had been so attracted to certain men. It was as if something deep in my being bonded with them. Once I knew what it was I was free.

A vision experience is the art of knowing or seeing things that are otherwise unknown or invisible, thoughts that exist in the deepest places within our memory or within the memory of the universe. Visions are visceral and passionate. Visions are the reward of the optimist, the adventurer. They are not available to the pessimist or those yearning for control.

Wisdom experiences were once thought to be limited to a few specialists within a community, a shaman, guru, priest, or physician who provided the channel for a community between higher and lower powers. Average people were excluded from access to the gods because they were considered unskilled, unaware, or unworthy.

Many people felt the visionary powers within themselves but had few skills for tapping into the information. Most of us are not raised with a tradition of visions but with a rejection of them. The only totem we were given at birth was a teddy bear. Those of us raised as part of a sensible, rational culture that denied intuitive knowledge are only now beginning to recognize other levels of memory, consciousness, and spiritual power.

In the past, individuals could seek some limited visions—the soldier making a personal connection to "the force" in battle, the young woman suddenly transformed by an appearance of the Virgin. Extrasensory or intuitive gifts have been accepted, but the practice of visioning was still limited to those uniquely trained or theologians for whom it was a vocation, a life commitment.

Now these paths to wisdom, toward "knowing," are available to all of us. Religious freedom, physical security, and material wealth allow more freedom for the spirit. We are able and encouraged to specialize in our own lives. We are exhorted daily to seek spiritual growth and deeper connections to the community. We are free to seek visions, to make these journeys into the light or dark.

The path and the process have been known by a few since the beginning of time. You can use the teachings of any of the world's great spiritual traditions—Christian, Judaic, Buddhist, Muslim, Native American, Hindu—because they all share similar steps and the same path.

There are guideposts. All the wisdom traditions provide instructions, restrictions, reassurance, and direction. The only essential that the pilgrim must have is a commitment to the process and a rock-solid belief in the power of what lies within your own heart and mind. You must trust the experience and truth of your intuitive gifts.

You can use these journeys to answer questions: "What should I do? What do I want? How do I feel?" You can use them to deepen your own self-knowledge: "What is truly important to me? Who am I? What is this feeling I always have within me?" You can use vision quests for business: "What would work? What is the weakness or the strength of this project?" They can be useful for family and relationship issues: "What is going wrong in my family? What part is each person playing? What would make the family work better? Who needs to change?"

Perhaps the most important use I have found in visioning is the chance to relax into one's best sources of information for anything. There is even information available to help us understand what is happening in the world and what will happen in the future.

The ways to embark on an inner journey are varied; there are a variety of styles within the wisdom traditions. You will have many choices. The basic vision path remains the same regardless of the steps you choose to take or whether you skip some steps. These are the twenty steps most common to the wisdom traditions.

1. *Awakening to the Need*
2. *Challenging the Present*
3. *Reaffirming Belief*
4. *Trusting in Self and Spirit*
5. *Clearing a Space*
6. *Physical Balance*
7. *Commitment to Simplicity*
8. *Feelings of Deep Rest*
9. *Elimination of Diversions*
10. *Balancing Rituals*

11. *Acceptance of Humility*
12. *State of Vulnerability*
13. *Clarifying the Mission*
14. *Choosing the Way*
15. *Finding the Sense*
16. *Asking and Receiving*
17. *Translating*
18. *Checking the Fit*
19. *Making the Commitment*
20. *Transformation*

You may want to take a journey in your mind alone, the armchair path. You may prefer to join a group—there are "New Age," more traditional religious, Native American, and academic groups available that explore these steps and prepare people for vision quests. You may want to seek a personal guide through your own spiritual tradition or church. Joseph Campbell, one of the great scholars and writers on myth and vision, said in his PBS series *The Power of Myth* that it is important to have a teacher for such intense experiences: "The difference is that the one who cracks up is drowning in the water in which the mystic swims. You have to be prepared for this experience."

Most of us like to start out with armchair journeys more than real ones, and that is a choice that this book fits well. You can just play around with any new ideas, insights, and possibilities you find. There are many worthwhile books on journeys toward the heart, and some are included in the acknowledgments section. There are only a few detailed guides and they require interpretation.

The ability to know your own destiny and character through a vision experience is empowering. Those who have done it consider it the most powerful of all human gifts. It is a power that can only be used for good. Spiritual or self-knowledge is always for the purpose of contributing to your world. Therefore, no religion and no spiritual tradition considered a vision quest valid unless the resulting awareness had value for the entire community. A person was considered crazy if his or her thoughts were for that person alone. A vision must have meaning beyond oneself to be honored.

I have been drawn down the vision path from my earliest memories. I can remember, at four, standing on the railroad tracks behind our small farm and knowing that I belonged to the world. My first lessons came from the animals and plants. I was raised as an Episcopalian and I loved the rituals of that faith but did not feel the Spirit. A sense of the possibilities of visioning settled within me at seventeen, when I sat in my first history class in college. I found this understanding deepened and concentrated when I chose the field of anthropology as a vocation.

I have since followed the vision steps I have learned and answered many of my most difficult and complex questions. I have also found answers to those things that sadden me about our society. The process has brought me deep understanding and peace. One can tap into the "source" or the "well" of the world. When you reach in to this collective wisdom you will find that all paths lead toward the center and that the center is a place of passion and safety.

CHAPTER I

AWAKENING TO THE NEED

There is always a temptation to cover the abyss with a trance.

—Marion Woodman

"There are two kinds of people," she once decreed to me emphatically.

One kind, you can just tell by looking at them at what point they congealed into their final selves. It might be a very nice self, but you know you can expect no more surprises from it. Whereas, the other kind keeps moving, changing....They are fluid. They keep moving forward and making new trysts with life, and the motion of it keeps them young. In my opinion, they are the only people who are still alive. You must be constantly on your guard, Justin, against congealing.

—Gail Godwin,
The Finishing School

Summer brings out such a feeling of being alive. There is so much light. It draws us out of ourselves and into the world. We are sometimes torn between taking a new risk, a swing forward where we reach our legs to the sun or ride it backward in the tuck position.

Many of us were raised in the tuck position. It is a protective stance. It reduces tension and pain by shutting down. We can avoid going to the edge. We can choose the hammock over the kayak, the television over the connection to a community. Summer confuses us.

We all need balance, we need to relax, but it's crucial to remember the backward movement is only a way to gather momentum. It is a misinterpretation to see risk as pain instead of the feeling of being fully alive. Your emotions will always align with your intentions.

Passion is not found in the moments of respite. It is in the quest, the forward stretch, the recognition of the light, your willingness to open. Breathe deeply on these beautiful days, untuck.

My mother apologized to me last year on Mother's Day. She told me she regretted not hugging me or playing with me when I was a child. She had been raised by a loving nanny, not her parents. It was the English way. She did not understand until her seventies that raising me without a nanny could mean anything.

Lots of parents find they have regrets these days because so much of what children want has changed. We once provided food, shelter, education, and an inheritance. We pushed our children hard so they would turn out better than we did. We left them money and property.

Now we live longer, inheritance is delayed, and our children earn their own way in the world. They want to feel better than we do, not just do better. The legacy we leave as parents is changing.

When today's young adults talk about what they wish their parents had given them, the answer is often support, in the form of someone wishing them well, and memories.

Losing your temper is a sure sign that you know you're in the wrong.

There is so much unsolved right now. There are many questions. What will happen in the world, in our country, and in our hearts? Rainer Maria Rilke wrote that we must "be patient towards all that is unsolved in our hearts. Try to love the questions themselves." They are like locked rooms or books that are written in a foreign tongue. The answers are unavailable because we are not ready to live them.

Instead of answers, there is another question. In the best of all possible worlds, what do I really want to happen?

Vision Step One:
Awakening to the Need

We are learning to live in two worlds: the mundane, mortal world we, as individuals, have become so accomplished at and the sacred, spiritual world that connects us deeply to our being. We are learning that there must be more to life than just increasing its speed.

The first step in any vision journey is one we have all felt many times. It is an opening within your heart and mind. It may feel like a small window that appears to show you a better way to do something or to think about someone. You have an experience, you are somehow touched, there is a shift in your body and your awareness. Energy seems to flow into you, and you feel a unique connection with life. It can be anything from a small creative breakthrough to a major philosophical shift.

I remember the first time I felt the possibility of a window into my world. I was ten, walking along the railroad tracks behind our house in the Spokane Valley. I looked down the tracks, saw an image of the future, and felt the pulse of the whole world. Another powerful opening was at seventeen, on the dormitory lawn at college, reading a book about evolution and suddenly realizing how closely all life is linked.

A man wrote to me recently describing his "awakening":

> A few years ago I experienced something which is very difficult to describe. A "happening" that was, in part, a sensation, but mostly a mental awareness, or perhaps a brief glimpse, of the knowledge and understanding of all things.
>
> It happened as I was walking in my backyard, and lasted only a few seconds, if that. My attention was drawn upward, and to the left, but I nei-

11

ther saw nor heard a thing. I stopped dead in my tracks, and to this day am not sure whether or not it was involuntary. I remember that my eyes were wide open and unblinking, and I experienced an effervescent sensation in the area above or around my head. It was as if a window in an invisible barrier had been opened for a brief moment, and at that time I had the knowledge of all things.

Many things can trigger these moments: the birth of a child, sunrise, sunset, the sound of the ocean, the smell of a forest, telepathic experiences, clairvoyance, immersion in music, dance, art, the power of a cathedral, near-death experiences, grief, falling in love, orgasm.

The stories of other lives can transform us. Books have always held a powerful place in my life as I read of foreign places, different lives, and new perceptions. Books are one way to connect with other sources and bring them into ourselves. I have always wanted to understand the values and belief systems of others so that I could understand my own. Traveling always creates an awakening.

Think back over your own moments when a window to the world opened: one day, on a fishing boat traveling to Alaska through the majesty of the fjords, your consciousness changed; one week in another country loosened your sense of right or wrong; a chance to rest resolved a problem.

An opening may have come through the resolution of childhood pain when you recovered your true self. You realized how much you had given up long ago in the trauma of being too young to validate your own experience. You became what seemed necessary for survival. Now you are independent.

The internal desire for greater understanding comes as life stretches us, as lessons are learned through pain or powerful experiences. We are often transformed in ways we feel but cannot label.

All of the wisdom traditions, including Christianity, describe such moments of enlightenment and encourage us to seek them. Satori, enlightenment, Nirvana, ecstasy, and ascension are all described as the loss of self in the feeling of oneness, the end to separation.

As I write this I am listening to the voice of Beverly Sills; the beauty brings tears to my eyes, and passion fills heart and body. There are so many ways to awaken. We open at different times and in different ways. It matters not how, just that you are here, you have heard, you cannot let it go.

The philosophers and prophets remind us that there is a voice in the universe that only you can hear, a voice that mythologists have labeled "the call." It is the call to value your own life. To make the choice of risk and bliss over the known and secure. Joseph Campbell, in his now famous PBS series, exhorted each of us to "follow our bliss."

You may choose not to hear your spirit. You may prefer to build a safe life within the compound of your own home or community, to avoid the risk. It is possible to find contentment, but not happiness, within such a familiar box. Many prefer a life of comfort and control.

You may choose, instead, to be open to new experiences, to leave the limits of familiarity and your conditioning, to hear the call. When you have heard the call then you must act. If you never hear it, perhaps nothing is lost. If you hear it and ignore it, your life is lost.

Try to track the windows that open for you. Try to trace your awakening. Take note of the moments when your understanding seems to take a leap. What do you think is drawing you to ask deeper and more difficult questions about your life and your community? You are not alone. We are each called to be our unique self because self-knowledge allows us to see and support others. American culture is searching for a "new story," a new way of seeing each other and our place in the world. It is, I believe, a peculiar need or secret of being human that we continually look for new ways to be. The individual recognition of self is a key experience.

CHAPTER II

CHALLENGING THE PRESENT

The road is better than the inn.

—Miguel Cervantes

I've never been much of a collector, just the odd geode or crystal or glass paperweight. I love anything that light can illuminate. Yet, now I am collecting snow globes. I pretend I don't know where they come from. Every time I turn around I have another one sitting somewhere in the house or office.

There are penguins in the snow, a wizard with a crystal ball that lights up, a frog on a rock, and a clown that juggles. The important part of all these is the snow part. It isn't always snow inside, sometimes it is colored flakes or sparkles.

Now I wonder how old snow globes are and if other people, in the past, have wanted an intact world that you could shake up and settle down. There is such predictability in these little environments, until they start to leak. I think my wizard is evaporating, his cap will soon be above water.

Being who I am, I have to analyze the inside story on this collection. Sigmund Freud would say it's a desire for control. The globe gives me the perfect world, chosen by me, maintained by me, that I can turn upside down depending on my whims. He would be right, I suppose.

I think it is my desire for paradise, a little bit of heaven, a memory, captured in time.

Intimacy, I see now, was what he feared the most;
intimacy made him uneasy, as if he had forfeited or
lost part of himself in the process, as if it had made
him vulnerable to criticism, to attack. I had seen his
face after I had once, in the early days (of our mar-
riage), prevailed on him to love me; it was fretful,
pained, resentful. All this I saw in one terrible
moment, as he turned away from me. He sat on the
edge of the bed, naked, his clasped hands hanging
between his knees. Poor Tom's a-cold, I thought. I
was so frightened then that I vowed I would keep my
distance. For that was what he wanted, and I still
loved him enough to try to please him.

—Anita Brookner,
Brief Lives

Don't keep your distance. The more intense the fear of
intimacy is, the more willing you must be to transcend it.

August is the month my mother visits. She lives in Arizona the rest of the year. Mom and her husband drive up with their trailer and park it about two hours away. That is just about the right distance from relatives for Mom to feel comfortable. I look forward to her visits because she is such a wonderful, eccentric spirit.

At the moment Mom is doubled over laughing, tears in her eyes. She has been opening the mail that she had forwarded to my office. One package is a certificate of award for a mail-order contest she entered and won a small prize.

The reason she is laughing is the second package she opened. It is a plastic frame for the certificate in the first package so she can hang it on the wall. Mom cannot believe that anyone anywhere would hang a mail-order contest certificate on the wall.

I start laughing with her when she describes the trip up here. They bought their usual secondhand car, put on a trailer hitch, hooked up the trailer, and lost the transmission fifty-one miles north of Prescott, where they live. The real problem was their pets: two large dogs, two cats, an aquarium of fish, and a cockatiel.

The dogs ride in the trailer living area with the cockatiel in a cage. The cats have to ride in the bathroom because the dogs chase them. The cockatiel cannot be in the same room as the cats for obvious reasons. When Mom leaves the trailer to visit me, the cats get the living room, the dogs stay outside, and the bird gets his freedom in the bathroom.

Switching the pets around is getting more difficult as she nears eighty. I am reminded of the chicken, the grain, and the fox that had to be ferried across a river in a boat that could hold only one at a time.

I took her to the new house we bought, and she insisted on climbing all the steps down to the beach and back. She did a fast review of the neighborhood and in seconds had spotted the closest Episcopal church. It was her usual reminder. "Look, dear, it's only a few blocks to church."

Last year she decided to write her life story. Lots of people decide that, but my mother did it in her usual matter-of-fact way. She enrolled in a community-college writing course, learned to use the computer at the public library, and wrote 150 pages. She had mailed me a copy, but now she brings the floppy disk out of her purse and gives it to me. Mom has no trouble learning new ways or thoughts.

The book contains only the bare framework of the family saga because my mother doesn't think anything she does is unusual enough to write about. Like all true eccentrics, she thinks she is an average person. She did change the names to protect us. Marge became Maggie, Godfrey is Geoff, Michael is Mark, and I am Jeannie. She changed the dogs' names, too, even though they are all dead. What Mom didn't write about is far more interesting than what she did write about.

Mom didn't write about winning a contest for the prettiest ankles on the beach at Brighton or being one of the first London policewomen. Her badge number was 99. She had an advanced belt in judo and met my father at Scotland Yard. He was a police officer, too.

She started dating him so she could get to work on time. When he was directing traffic in her neighborhood he would see her barreling down the road on her bicycle, always late, and stop her. When she agreed to go out with him, he would stop all the other traffic and let her through.

Mom was a great athlete and is interested in everything. She used to brag about beating my father at tennis when she was nine months pregnant. She had a love of farming and chickens that led, in part, to our immigrating to Spokane, sponsored by distant relatives who owned a chicken ranch. My mother could wring a chicken neck the way she did everything else, without fuss.

She is a hard worker who took courses in America to move from bookkeeper to accountant to comptroller to office manager. She raised vegetables, kept cows, pigs, horses, and chickens, bowled, played the piano, sang with Sweet Adelines, and still sings in the church choir. Mom taught Sunday school and loves to dance.

She belongs to the American Business Women's Association and the Daughters of the British Empire. She laughs now that some of the younger members of DBE want to change "Empire" to "Commonwealth" but the older ones won't let them.

Mom went skiing alone at forty just to try it, learned the hula at fifty, scootered through Europe in an orange jumpsuit at sixty, and bought herself a Harley-Davidson motorcycle at seventy. She gave up her horse because it had thrown her off once too often and joined a motorcycle club called the Retreads. She was elected senior queen at a nudist jamboree in her seventies.

I have a photo of her doing the Charleston at seventy-two. I have one of her some years later putting the last bricks on the chimney of a three-story house she helped build in the woods of northern Idaho. She still swims every day at seventy-seven. None of this is in the book because she assumes everyone does these things.

As I watch her walk onto the Vashon Ferry to go back to the trailer in Port Townsend, with her slight tilt from a bad hip, I realize what a wonderful model she has set for me. A model of freedom, optimism, adventure, aging, and opportunity. I feel lucky that it is August, she is here, still the same one-of-a-kind woman, and that she is my mother.

Vision Step Two:
Challenging the Present

At certain points in our lives, sometimes in times of crisis we decide to challenge the present. Many cultures have rites of passage or initiation in which you are expected to question your self and your reality. There are certain changes in a life that require information, guidance, ritual, and support. We need a boost to the next phase or stage. We need validation of what is happening.

We have few initiation rituals in America, and most of us need more thoughtful transitions from one age to another. We are beginning to treat midlife passage as one of these special times of review. It is considered a time to look at the first half of your life in order to decide what you will value for the last half.

The Plains Indians used one form of the vision quest as a mark of the movement from boy to warrior. You were expected to stretch your senses into another world, to gain the strength of a "totem" animal. You were then invincible and could do battle. A young man went into the hills for many days alone. He might deny himself food and water until his spirit came. He might sacrifice a finger joint if all else failed.

After successfully seeing or hearing his "spirit animal," he would return home with a special song to be sung in times of fear or a symbol of his communion and lifetime linkage with his totem. Many Indian names are drawn from the time of a child's first vision experience.

A male who could not achieve a successful warrior initiation and hunting quest might spend his life as a *berdache*, a male dressed as a female. These "specialists" took an alternative, nonviolent vision, a more philosophical or spiritual path to the vision experience.

The *berdache* was thought to have special powers because he had both male power and female intuition. His female qualities were seen as an inner power, the knowledge of love and his maleness as an outer power connecting him to the spirit world. The medicine man and the *berdache* were often the tribal specialists in the pursuit of visions. They taught their people how to pursue higher and deeper awareness.

A vision seeker could use any problem or feeling to mount a quest. The wisdom traditions of cultures are very similar in their definitions of external and internal power and in the vision steps they outline for those who want knowledge. Human beings are more alike than different at their core. We emphasize separation so often in our spiritual dialogues that we forget the obvious connections.

Many cultures no longer teach the history, the experience, the skills of the vision quest, so generations grow up with no understanding of the stirrings they feel at different times in their lives. We make up names for the obvious passages: baptism, confirmation, adolescence, menarche, birthday, first holy communion, Bar Mitzvah, *quinceanera*, menopause, retirement.

Most modern humans begin to challenge the present when something less obvious than a birthday jolts them into confronting their existing environment or their current reality. Usually a perceived failure creates instability somewhere in our life. The balance has been disrupted, the harmony of whatever plateau we had previously reached is lost. Divorce, work problems, illness, or other losses somehow shake up our settled routine. Divine discontent creates anxiety, perhaps depression, grief, or illness, and we realize we must reexamine what we thought was under control. There may be little information available on what the problems are, just dissatisfaction, a loss of passion, or a feeling of disconnection from our life force. There may be more information and evidence that we are in transition than we want to confront, especially if our body is showing its own signs of discontent.

Each of us gets strong signals when it is time to do personal homework. You already may be less resistant to illness, losing sleep, seeing a counselor, examining a new religion, reading, struggling with your thoughts, going to a class, or joining some new leader you think might have the answers.

If you know what your questions are, write them down. If you cannot identify your questions, it is time to ask yourself about the content and quality of your life to ascertain the level of challenge or discontent you really feel.

Go through your weekly and monthly schedule and highlight in your favorite color those activities that brought you some kind of pleasure or satisfaction. Highlight in a color that is not your favorite those activities you would rather not have done. Leave the neutral activities neutral. Even though many of us have to do things we don't like in order to pay our bills or be good citizens, you should be able to see, in color, what kind of negative and positive balance you have in your schedule. What are you willing to change?

Create a circle and divide it into three sections: individual, life work, and relationships. How does your time and energy get divided up in this pie? There is no reason for them to be equal. If you are starting a new job, that wedge may be the largest. If you are ill, the individual wedge will be important while you concentrate on getting better. If you are raising small children, your relationship section will be the largest. Within the sections you can create as many subdivisions as you like:

- INDIVIDUAL: physical; intellectual; emotional; spiritual.

- LIFE WORK: paid work; creative work; community work; home maintenance; recreation.

- RELATIONSHIPS: family; relatives; friends; colleagues; neighbors; support professionals (physician, dentist, counselor, lawyer, etc.).

The pie diagram and its various wedges become a balance wheel* of your life that you can use to ask questions about what you are actually doing. You can see how you are spending your time and energy. You can compensate for perceived imbalance among the sections of the circle by knowing it is what you prefer. We all have self-selected strengths and weaknesses. Loving your work can take you through some lonely times. Friends or a lover can help you when work falls apart.

Ask yourself, "Why am I doing what I'm doing? Does it bring me satisfaction or passion? Is it enough? What are my alternatives?" Can you list five alternative ways of making a living, five places in which you could live outside of the state you now live in, five sources of love and support other than the individuals or groups you now rely on? How safe do you feel?

What have been your biggest mistakes? What would you change if you had only a year to live? Do you know what you truly want? Imagine others discussing you, thinking you cannot hear them. What would you like to overhear them saying about you? What do you want to be able to believe about yourself? How has this changed over time? What is truly important to you? What has heart for you? What is the one thing that you are doing that will have impact beyond your life?

There are many ways to challenge the present and it is often an automatic process—you sense you must change. Start asking the questions, listening to the responses in your body, reading, walking, and talking with your friends. Slow down your external life, simplify as much as possible. The answers to your questions travel slowly and sometimes the questions take even longer. They must be able to catch up with you.

Challenging the present takes you into a future chosen by you, unique to you. Scout the terrain of your life. We move forward by going deeper.

*Alene Moris, a Seattle-based career counselor, first created the "balance wheel" concept and shared it with me.

CHAPTER III

REAFFIRMING BELIEF

*The fact is that the mad rush of the last hundred years
has left us out of breath. We have had no time to
swallow our spittle. We know that the automated
machine is here to liberate us and show us the way
back to Eden; that it will do for us what no revolution,
no doctrine, no prayer, and no promise could do. But
we do not know that we have arrived. We stand there
panting, caked with sweat and dust afraid to realize
that the seventh day of the second creation is here, and
the ultimate sabbath is spread out before us....*

— Eric Hoffer,
The Temper of Our Times

Life is a free-wheeling vendor if you are willing to receive. There is a natural harmony if you give up the illusion of control. Accept ambivalence, embrace confusion; you have time. Let go, let it unfold, let it happen. The child within is safe. The adult is free to play.

Changed plans are dancing lessons from the universe.

The holiest spot on Earth is where an ancient hatred is replaced by a present love.

—Tara Singh,
The Course in Miracles

Bill Moyers hosted a PBS special recently on hate. One of those interviewed talked of "messianic moments." He referred to moments when all life is one, when the spirit of the Messiah seems truly present. Moments like that change you forever because they change you on a visceral level.

You can see in people's faces and hear in their voices whether they have been visited by enough of these moments. Some faces are pinched, closed, wary, vigilant, ready to attack with words or fists. Others are open, optimistic, looking for good, not the bad. It is more than just the optimist/pessimist view of life; it is an acceptance or rejection of life.

When times are troubled, it is important to maximize your possibilities for a moment or visitation. Margaret Mead called it enlightenment—experiences that open your eyes, your mind, and your heart. In the 1950s Mead offered these internal ways to enlightenment:

- teaching or being with young children while the spirit is still intact within them;

- raising animals, because they teach us about life and compassion;

- recovering from a life-threatening illness, accident, or depression and clearing up your priorities;

- being psychoanalyzed to extend self-knowledge;

- surviving a love affair with an old Russian.

There are also many external ways to give yourself the messianic touch: listening to songbirds, rescuing ladybugs, walking through the Pike Place Market, hiking Mount Rainier, watching sea otters, smelling roses and freesias, riding ferries, eating cherries, and napping in the sun. Add your own. Seek out the antidote to hate and anger by deepening your love of life.

Heroes and heroines move out of the society that would have protected them, and into the dark forest; into the world of fire, of original experience. Original experience has not been interpreted for you, and so you've got to work out your life for yourself. Either you can take it or you can't. You don't have to go far off the interpreted path to find yourself in very difficult situations. The courage to face the trials and to bring a whole new body of possibilities into the field of interpreted experience for other people to experience—that is the hero's deed.

—Joseph Campbell,
The Power of Myth

Vision Step Three:
Reaffirming Belief

I am often asked why people can be so preoccupied with understanding and changing their life and their self. I answer that we, as a culture, are hungry for passion. We are hungry for a more intense connection with our life force. We once filled this need with the search for food and shelter. We are no longer satisfied by just multiplying floor space and supplies. We are now freer to ask about the quality of our lives, so we do.

The questions we asked in the past centered on, "Will I have enough to eat?" not "Will I eat too much?" Once the stomach is full, many more of us are drawn to the search for understanding. It is no longer enough to be successful; we want to feel successful. We want internal as well as external satisfaction.

There are so many barriers in our culture to the joy, peace, and passion we are told is available that you need to know clearly what you are willing to let yourself have. There are many moments of testing what you believe you can have in this life. If the bliss of clearly knowing the direction of your life feels like more than you can handle or enjoy, then you will block out the questions and the answers.

There are personal and cultural barriers you will need to clear away to affirm your belief in the information and energy that are available to you through a vision journey.

Childhood pain is often the central barrier to adult joy. Alice Miller in her books writes of the separation from genuine self that occurs when a powerless child tries to find ways to survive in a family that is unsafe. Marion Woodman writes of the loss of the feminine heart in women as they compete in a male world. Robert Bly speaks of the loss of trust in the "wildman" power of men.

Sheldon Kopp writes, "You must plow the fields of your past so that you can plant your own crops." Do your homework. Read, talk, join a group, seek counseling or guidance. Know what you can about yourself, your masculinity, your femininity, your shadow side, so that you can trust your intuitive gifts. Do a family history or a three-generation genealogy so you know your past.

Check the messages of your family, your culture, the environment you were raised in—not just what people told you they believed in, but how they actually behaved. You need to know. There are many biases in American culture against this research, against intuition and self-knowledge. There are also biases against self-esteem and independence. Which perceptions and values that you hold have you been socialized into, and which have you chosen for yourself? Do you know what your priorities are and what you truly believe in?

Watch out for traps like the "theory of retribution," the idea that the gods are not on your side but are, in fact, competitors. This theory suggests that one should fear and placate the powers in the universe because, like us, they may be jealous and territorial.

Retribution takes us back to our earliest cultural experiments with religion. Early humans sought explanations for weather, accidents, life, and death as we do. Animism, the belief that all things have spirits, provided many explanations that science now provides for us. Each object or power in the universe was given a personality, a transference of what a man knew about himself to a spirit. The gods had to be satisfied, as powerful men and women did, if the rest of the tribe were to be allowed to prosper.

The sun god, the fertility god, the rain god, and the spirits of game animals all had to be rewarded and treated with reverence. If you wanted something, you had to give up something. Give the gods 10 percent of your crop or a sacrificial lamb, heart, or virgin, and you could safely keep the rest. We made deals, and in our psyche some of us still think we have to. We feel that too much joy or passion will invite the displeasure of others or of God, so we are careful to limit ourselves and our pleasures. We hide our light under a basket.

Participation in a vision quest requires you to believe that the powers of the universe are not only on your side but also within you. You must feel deeply that passion is your genuine life force and ecstasy your inheritance. You deserve all that you are, all that you will allow yourself to feel. We give to others from the overflow within us, not the emptiness. "Self-knowledge is for the purpose of contributing."

Rigid religious systems also limit vision because they close off sources of information. Some religions hold that only the experts can have transforming experiences. A religion or a religious leader that reduces an individual's faith in himself or herself shrinks instead of expands the possibilities. How open is your belief system? How much have you changed over the past decade? Do you read and think about religious traditions other than your own?

Any rigid system of thought—political, scientific, psychological, economic, or philosophical—limits access to information and growth. It is possible to value highly and believe in a structure and at the same time be open to new perceptions and thoughts. How available is your mind?

Family visions are also powerful barriers. Adult children of alcoholics carry a legacy of an unsafe world that requires control, perfectionism, vigilance, and defense. Their protection of self often eliminates the openness and trust essential to vision. Pessimists do not believe in the power, or they believe it to be negative. Check your family perspective. Clarify the vision of the world that you have inherited.

Write down your beliefs about life and compare them to what you think is your father's or mother's perceptions. You may have some personal homework to do before you will be able to stretch beyond the framework laid out in your family's patterns.

Reaffirming belief in the goodness and power within you, being able to feel them, is essential to the trust in the universe necessary to tap into all its resources. All you need you will find within.

CHAPTER IV

TRUSTING IN SELF AND SPIRIT

*The human spirit is virtually indestructible, and its
ability to rise from the ashes remains as long as the
body draws breath.*

—Alice Miller,
For Your Own Good

Reading the newspaper or hearing the news can jolt your senses. Changes at work and home sometimes leave us struggling to understand and accommodate. Our personal experiences and perceptions frequently need updating. Values we've held forever might be questioned. It is this confusion, this questioning that make us human. The spirit is being redefined.

How do we hold on when all around us seems chaos? Hold on to what you know deep within you. Hold on to your inner sense of honor and integrity. It is easier to handle change when something within you is changeless.

Why do you never find anything written about that idiosyncratic thought you avert to, about your fascination with something no one else understands? Because it is up to you. There is something you find interesting, for a reason hard to explain. It is hard to explain because you have never read it on any page; there you begin. You were made and set here to give voice to this, your own astonishment.

—Annie Dillard

Sometimes we are intimidated instead of exhilarated by our individuality. We hold back our thoughts or interests, thinking them unworthy if not validated by others. We assume because it is our curiosity alone that it is inherently suspect.

Cherish your uniqueness; there is magic in being peculiar, weird, eccentric. It means you can hear your own voice among the almost overwhelming buzz of this world.

Creativity isn't optional—it's a survival skill.

Changing times require creativity because it enhances the ability to see alternatives. New ideas are this decade's most important raw material. You need to be able to look at the same problem as everyone else and come up with a different solution.

Creative people:

- pay attention to and nurture their ideas;

- give up on conformity;

- make lots of mistakes;

- break routines—change colors, routes, foods, smells, exercise;

- become international citizens because ideas come from everywhere;

- entertain the absurd;

- frequently play like children;

- take a break, leave time to dream;

- sleep on it.

Just relaxing will expand your intelligence. These are the activities that help us discover the elements that link us together. Creativity is part of your human spirit. It gives you joy, uniqueness, and a key to the future if you will allow it.

A Child of the Universe

by Alberta Stone*

I believe I was born into this world asking questions, looking for light. I've always been curious about life, its meaning, and my purpose for being here.

Even as a teenager I had a thirst for spiritual knowledge. This hunger continued throughout my university education. I was certain through my social-work career that I was going to help many people but I learned I couldn't control the universe. My expectations of myself and others were unrealistic.

I then began an earnest journey involving many paths. It has been said that when the pupil is ready, the teacher will come. I was open, eager, and needy.

A good friend introduced me to a teacher, Dr. Fritz Kunkel, a German psychiatrist who was a pioneer in combining religion and psychology. When he came to Seattle for a week's seminar, I attended every class. It was a turning point in my life.

Three of the prescriptions he gave for the spiritual journey were enthusiasm (commitment), a big notebook, and lots of patience. Years later, I still have enthusiasm, stacks of notebooks, and I'm always working on patience. I learned that humor and the ability to make changes are absolute necessities.

I became an archaeologist of the Spirit—digging for more and more understanding. I studied many religions, philosophies, and metaphysics. Most helpful of all were years of seminars in Jungian psychology. These studies opened up doors of deeper self-realization. I learned how our unconscious energies can be

*Alberta (Bertie) Ramsey Stone is a retired social worker and a graduate of the University of Washington. She has been married fifty years and has two daughters and four grandchildren. She has worked with Jennifer's Community Service Committee for over nine years.

integrated into our conscious personality with an awareness of the opposites in our nature. We cannot deny any part of our personality if it is to be understood and transformed.

I am a Christian. My husband and I have attended the same church for forty years. We have been participants in both giving and receiving. I love my church, but it has not been enough to feed my spirit completely. None of the other paths I have pursued has distracted me from my faith. They have expanded and enriched it. I consider myself a "child of the universe"—not boxed into any particular category.

The greatest discovery of all during these searching years has been to know that the answers I sought were within myself. Jesus, I feel, was the greatest psychiatrist who ever lived because he understood our humanness and our Divine Spirit. He knew what he was talking about when he told us, "The Kingdom of God is within. Seek and you shall find." I now know that all the questions don't need to be answered. Some of life is meant to be a mystery.

The best part of all is knowing that I am not alone on this journey. The Source of my Being is always there to hold me up like the power of eagle wings even when I sometimes feel I haven't earned or deserved it. I have only to recognize and acknowledge that power. The choice is mine.

I am still a student. Sometimes I get to be the teacher. The exchange of ideas and experiences with others never ceases to be stimulating to me. I have tried to live my life in balance. I have parented two loving daughters and have a marriage of fifty years.

My travels to other countries have given me a sense of kinship with other cultures. I have always worked at a wide variety of both paid and volunteer jobs. My life's tapestry has been colorful, with deep shadows of pain and disillusionments blended with many blessings. Every experience has been a teacher.

I don't like the aging process I now face and the physical limitations it can bring when life for me has always been so full.

Thankfully, my spiritual path holds no limitations, and that continues to be comforting and challenging. I know there will be more changes, which I hope I can embrace with grace and understanding. When I make my transition, I feel it will be another graduation from one school to another.

I have found that once a spiritual journey starts there is no turning back. There is no ending, only new beginnings. Light is light wherever you find it.

Vision Step Four:
Trusting in Self and Spirit

Review your responses to change and crisis. It is very difficult to trust the information available in the natural universe unless you trust yourself. Now is the time to review your past responses to change and crisis.

Think back over your life and ask these questions: How open do you feel you are to change? How able have you been to follow your intuitive judgments? Are you good at deciding what is safe and what is not safe for you? Are you more likely to follow what is offered by a leader, or do you sift possibilities through your own experience and values? Look back over your life and decide how good you are at basic survival skills. How has life turned out for you?

The more you know about yourself, your strengths and weaknesses, the more you will be able to contribute to your community. The more clearly you establish your values, the more awareness you have of your own behavior, the more able you are to understand others, the easier it becomes to affirm yourself on any personal journey.

The basis of self-knowledge is an awareness of what you believe to be your value in this world. What do you think you deserve? Do you consider yourself to be a good person? How much joy can you feel comfortable with? Are you able to resist the demands of others when they don't correspond to your own rights and needs? How able are you to be generous with others out of your own sense of abundance? How well do you take care of your intellectual, emotional, spiritual, and physical self?

When you have faced crisis, trauma, or tragedy, how have you fared? Would you describe yourself as a survivor? Are you usually optimistic, confident, independent, and determined?

How well do you recover from disappointment, injustice, unexpected events, or changes precipitated by the decisions of others?

Can you travel long distances or in other cultures alone and feel secure? Have you hiked or spent time in a cabin or tent isolated from others? What have you been able to do by yourself throughout your life? What is easy for you to do alone? What is hard? Do you need a witness to an emotional insight or a sunset to validate your pleasure and understanding?

When you are alone and quiet inside, do memories sometimes flood your consciousness? Can you still feel an event from another time? Can you breathe into these emotions and let them move gently toward resolution? Are you able to let go of the past and any pain it represents? Can you accept and see the humor in so many of your beliefs and so much of your behavior? You are making the choices, not always of events, but of the way you respond to them.

Most of us are experienced survivors in the mundane, practical, mortal world, but we have little experience with the sacred, eternal, spiritual, mystical, magical, unusual world. We can feel the knowledge within us but have few skills for accepting it.

Review any spontaneous experiences you have had (unexpected knowing, telepathy, insight, intuition, altered consciousness, communion with nature or another person, powerful connections to music, art, the world, the Spirit, a sense of harmony, a moment of compassion).

Have you had passionate, visceral, opening events in your life and been able to accept the vulnerability? The dawn of a new day, the birth of a child, the beauty of the world, the feeling of community, the sudden elimination of a separation between you and others, all can be transcending, transforming experiences.

Decide what kinds of preparation will strengthen both your ability to be open and your self-discipline. Talk to friends, teachers, or the spiritual guides you trust. Read in your areas of interest. This book provides useful exercises. Eugene Gendlin's book *Focusing* also provides a specific series of exercises to help you build trust in yourself and your intuitive spirit. There are other books available that will stretch your belief in self. There are classes, seminars, and counselors.

Look at the religious traditions you are part of and see what information and paths are offered. Watch out for limits. Religions tend to name things; spirituality never does. Churches resist letting their members experience God directly. They pose as intermediaries who have the only way or connection and leave you powerless.

Many tribal cultures ascertain your readiness for a vision journey by measuring your faith. One of the experienced and powerful leaders would assign special tests of endurance and skill. You can seek a leader or guide or devise your own tests and then grant yourself permission to continue along the path.

Only you can decide what kind of journey you want to take and under what circumstances. Turn to your community for support and clarification. You can join an organized group that schedules journeys such as Vision Trek, a group located in Oregon. A key issue is that you feel safe talking to yourself on a deeper level. If your first experiences are worthwhile, it will be easier to test yourself alone in the future.

Personal journeys are ways of sensing our destiny ourselves. They require a connection with self and the courage to follow the truth within you. There is no passion or vision in being someone else.

CHAPTER V

CLEARING A SPACE

The hungry psyche has replaced the empty belly.

—Robert Ardrey

Solitude

by Charlotte Bottoms*

Reference books use solitude and loneliness as synonyms; antonyms would be more appropriate. Solitude is the willful choice of being alone—a time for reflection and introspection. Loneliness is being sad from want of companionship or sympathy.

There are different names for solitude: R and R, time out, or retreat. It is a period of time, however brief or extended, when one is free from the cares and worries of daily living. It is a time for rebuilding the spirit, a time of inner strength and peace.

In the country you can listen to the sounds of nature, birds, animals, water, wind, and quietness. Cities offer more of a challenge for finding solitude, but such places do exist there.

There are elements of our society that say being alone is antisocial, however moments of solitude can be very precious. There is an exhilaration of the spirit, an ecstasy of the mind. It is good for the soul!

---

*Charlotte Bottoms, a graduate of the University of Nebraska, is a retired teacher who has done volunteer work with Jennifer and the Community Service Committee for over nine years. In 1990 she spent eight months as a volunteer purser and medical records technician aboard the *Tole Mour*, a 156-foot sailing ship that provided health care in the Marshall Islands.

Charlotte has two married daughters and three grandchildren. Her hobbies include walking with her golden retriever, pinochle, reading, gardening, and embroidery.

Guilt is not meeting the expectations of others, imagined or real.

Guilt follows many of us around on any day, but the thought of holidays can make it multiply.

It's an uncomfortable feeling, hard to identify, which we assign to ourselves or willingly accept from others, even strangers.

Give yourself a break; reduce the shame, fear, and tensions from irrational guilt. Check out the sources of your self-blame. If you have violated your own standards of integrity, find a way to atone, a penance to free you.

When the source of your guilt comes from others, examine their expectations carefully and decide how much power you want to give away.

You can choose your way of life and resist, confront, forgive, or pass by those who would take it from you by small and large insults to your being. Shift their words out of your consciousness. This is a time to regenerate, clarify, and claim the integrity you possessed at the first moment of life.

There are many reasons that it is hard to stand alone. One is the need for witnesses to our own life. A strong feeling hits us and we turn for someone to share it with or validate it. A beautiful scene lies before us and it seems to offer less if other eyes don't see it, too.

Why can't we feel and see with the same intensity alone? Or is it too intense so we look to others to dilute the power? Are we the victims of too much romance and not enough joy? Sunsets that are for two, not one? How many moments of passion slip by because the right number is not present?

It is possible both to share and not share. It is possible to enjoy the music with companions and to go deeper, to hear the oboe, alone.

I said to my soul, be still, and wait without hope
For hope would be hope for the wrong thing; wait without love
For love would be love of the wrong thing; there is yet faith
But the faith and the love and the hope are all in the waiting.
Wait without thought, for you are not ready for thought:
So the darkness shall be the light, and the stillness the dancing.

—T. S. Eliot,
"East Coker" (Four Quartets)

When you get to be older and the concerns of the day have all been attended to and you turn to the inner life …Well, if you don't know where it is, you'll be sorry.

—Joseph Campbell,
The Power of Myth

Vision Step Five:
Clearing a Space

Vacations, retreats, sabbaticals, and initiations are geared toward achieving a renewal or transformation of self. They give us time, space, and a new environment to see things in a different way. All of the wisdom traditions send the pilgrim off on a trail, leave them alone on a mountain or in a special place or use sights, sounds, or drugs to create a nonordinary reality or trance.

Some Basque communities take a child at four to a sacred place and leave her alone all night to make her first contact with the world as a separate individual. It is a place the child has visited many times in the daylight with his or her parents. It is thought that each person must early in life make his or her personal relationship with God.

When the child is fourteen they go to a hut in the mountains to stay alone for six months and solidify their connections to the earth and the Spirit. Usually they see no one but in some cases there is another adolescent in a hut within walking range. The child chosen for the other hut is usually the one whom you least liked as you were growing up.

It's clear that most people do not go on a mystical journey while in a common place. Religions have always created inspiring places, or used drugs like peyote and alcohol that create a separation from regular time and space. Since I am writing only of journeys without drugs, I will emphasize the ability to separate, to change position without altering your conscious reality. The hardest step in most quests is deciding to take the time. Busyness is one of the ways we keep intuitive information at bay. Clearing space for the information of the heart or the power of nature requires severance from other activities that we may lean on for security and self-worth. It feels like a deprivation when we go into a different environment until we adjust, or unless we welcome the change.

American culture has few traditions for clearing a space. Many other societies have formal requirements for life review every seven to ten years. They expect you to think deeply about your life and make changes. They have retreat centers. Many groups believe that time spent in solitude is the most valuable time of one's life.

We think there is a shortage of time because we move and think so fast. We always have the feeling we are late, years late, or that we will run out of time. You are not late. You have plenty of time. You are going to live one hundred years. The question to ask is about the quality of those years.

There are well-known elements that contribute to the clearing of a space within your mind. There are many books and classes on meditation. Those practiced at meditations or vision journeys may be able to create the same environment; others must seek in the mountains, in their own home.

Most wisdom traditions feel that you must leave your home. They believe that environmental beauty is essential to clearing a space because it reminds you quickly of the power of nature, the harmony, the natural order of things. Whether you are walking beside the ocean and feeling the centuries of tides or sitting in the shadows deep in a virgin forest, you can feel the forces that surround you.

What kind of physical setting frees your mind, your heart, your creative energy? This is the setting you should seek.

Solitude is vital to this experience. You must learn to feel safe alone. The presence of someone else, particularly someone you know, often prevents you from being able to relax into yourself, your own values, and your intuitive center. The time you will allow yourself alone, to think about what you value, is a measure of the depth of your character.

CHAPTER VI

PHYSICAL BALANCE

Your life is not your master. It is your child.

—Pat Rodegast and Judith Stanton,
Emmanuel's Book

Sometimes as I have sat in the audience watching Martha Graham dance, it has seemed to me as if she were unwrapping our body image which has been tied up so long with the barbed wires of fear and guilt and ignorance and offering it back to us: a thing of honor.

Freeing at last, our concept of Self. Saying to us, the body is not a thing of danger, it is a fine instrument that can express not only today's feeling and activities, but subtle, archaic experiences, memories which words are too young in human affairs to know the meaning of.

—Lillian Smith,
The Journey

I have a theory about what is inside us. I think our bodies are factories full of teams of tiny people.

I got this idea when I was ten, while watching a film in school. It was called Hemo The Magnificent, and it was about the bloodstream. I felt intense during this film, realizing my body was full of red-cell guys swimming downstream, white cell guys struggling upstream, and lots of workers opening and closing the valves. I decided it was important to treat all the corpuscles with respect.

I kept this idea with me until, as an adult, I saw Woody Allen's *Everything You Wanted To Know About Sex*. He has a scene in which the sex cells, dressed as astronauts, are waiting to go on their mission. They are nervous, worried about whether they can do a good job, who will win the race to the egg, male or female. I realize how hard it is for some of the little people, being on call with little warning of when they will need to get into high gear.

Kissing is important because it wakes them up slowly, rolls them out of their hammocks and gives them time to get dressed and psyched up. A quickie exhausts them and gives them all headaches. They are less willing to get their act together next time.

My ideas about the little people have multiplied. I started to watch what I ate because the stomach people had such a messy job. They had to navigate their kayaks around all that stuff and add just the right amount of acid. I didn't want them in a toxic environment.

I can imagine them complaining about their working conditions: "Can you believe she is eating another cheeseburger? Last week I got my paddle stuck in a Twinkie." It hurts me to hear them fussing.

There are balloon squads who wait at the edge of your nose for air and race with it to the lungs. They are so busy that it's not surprising your nose sometimes gets messy. When you blow you need to be careful or you will hurt them. That is what nose hairs are for, something for them to hang on to when you sneeze. A sneeze is a tornado to one of the little air-moving people.

The air movers in the lungs are usually mellow. They prefer to wear pink sweatshirts and puff about endlessly. But when I am in a smoky environment, I can sense almost immediately that their pink shirts are turning brown and they are looking at themselves, upset.

They have long conversations late at night trying to decide what to do.

The heart guys work the hardest of anyone, and they are carefully selected and trained. They get to wear special uniforms. They work in teams of four that rotate every few hours. You put in a few months, and then you get to transfer to some slower area like the rear end.

The brain is a large, round room with a dome and a fireplace in the middle. The cells are arranged on cots or chairs in concentric circles around the fire. They muse a lot, read a lot; it is generally quiet. There are occasional well-mannered arguments among friends. A few of the younger ones cause trouble with radical thoughts, but it is more of an old girls' club than a free-for-all.

Once in a while one or two of them run amok, screaming that the sky is falling. The rest have to get up, run to the distressed team members, and calm them down. They sometimes have to call the memory cells out of their caves in the back of the room, to provide additional information so facts and common sense can prevail.

When I am sad I can see them all lying around, moping. They let the fire go out, close the windows so it is dark, and stop reading or talking. I get the message that they need exercise, but no one will move. Finally one of the wisdom cells, in a long white robe, gives them a gentle lecture, and they all light the fire and have tea.

Everyone loves massage. All the little people from top to bottom stretch out, serene smiles on their faces, waiting for their turn. If you miss one, it will complain until enough signals are sent to command attention. Promises are made during massages; contracts are signed. Each team vows to take better care of each other. They have sing-alongs and humming contests.

I've been much healthier since I accepted the theory of the little people. I listen to them carefully. Right now the stomach guys are resting, and the feet people are on their tiny pogo sticks, with their periscopes wanting to go out.

I am ready to please all of them. They take good care of me, and I give them anything they want.

Let's begin with a perversion so common that we consider it the normal condition of human beings—anhedonia (the insensitivity to pleasure, the incapacity for experiencing happiness). An anthropologist from another galaxy studying the ways of earthlings would probably look at our habit of warfare, our propensity to chronic anxiety and worry, our tendency to be motivated by guilt and shame, our obsession with work, our creating of stress and psychosomatic illness, and conclude that the human race has a love affair with pain. It is a rare person who is able to tolerate three uninterrupted days of happiness! We are most deeply threatened not by the fires of hell, but by the pleasures of paradise. Clearly, the earth is rich enough in resources to allow us pleasure, prosperity, and peace. Instead, we choose superfluous suffering. We manufacture surplus pain in quantities far greater than would be imposed upon us by our biological nature.

—Sam Keen,
The Passionate Life

Vision Step Six:
Physical Balance

The vision journey is both internal and external. The body as well as the spirit is involved. The ability to feel or hear the intelligence of your body and its memories is a very important survival skill and the foundation of most visions.

Eugene Gendlin refers to the body as a "biological computer generating these enormous collections of data and delivering them to you instantaneously when you call them up or when they are called up by some external event."

One of my signals or senses is to "listen to my stomach" because it will tell me the truth. We all have physical auras although it is difficult to sense our own. We usually can quickly pick up the aura of another person. We can read the signals of safety or danger.

We are so good at concealing our own aura from ourselves that we do not even realize that others know things about us that we do not know. Counselors often act as mirrors for the obvious. When our defenses break down through choice, relaxation, or grief we can see clearly and it often hurts.

The individual, in trying to break past his or her present reality or sense of self, may use exhaustion as a way of breaking through to the other side. The marathon encounter groups of the 1960s used that model. Many traditional and mythological quests required that both body and mind be extended to their utmost limits.

I believe that the same breakthrough to a new perception can be achieved through acceptance and love of your body. One way to reach acceptance is through physical balance. Find the most comfortable sense that you can within your own physical being.

Your body will become a distraction if it is not comfortable.

You know what works best for you, but most journeys start with a cleansing and soothing of the body as well as the mind. Many tribes and clans use special scents and colors to create balance and a signal to the gods that you are ready.

Clean everything you want to. Clip, cut, rearrange until you feel ready. Wear clothing made of natural fibers that are loose and provide no maintenance problems. That is why gurus always seem to prefer flowing robes. They are just more comfortable for lounging around.

Many traditions cleanse the body internally as well with fasting, sweat baths, aromas, purifiers, special emetics, or herb mixtures. You can take care of your food needs in any simple way but it seems important to exclude alcohol, coffee, overly processed foods, sugars, and any mind-altering substances. Review your basic needs so that your body can cooperate and concentrate on feeling instead of food, temperature, and comfort.

Acceptance of the body requires a further step. Many addicts or uncomfortable eaters are trying to fill a void within. They may create a sufficient defense that they cannot even feel, let alone accept their body. The emptiness does not always show but you will know it is there.

Sometimes it helps to do an inventory of what you like and don't like about your physical body. Ask yourself what you are willing to change and what you will probably not change. Make your peace with whatever it is you don't like. Your body does not have to be a monument to the pain, problems, or negatives that you have collected.

Let your body be free. You can always go back to the cramped or abused positions later. Take a deep breath, put the negative aside, and take the body that is you down the path.

CHAPTER VII

COMMITMENT TO SIMPLICITY

You will know your next step from this step.

I was walking in the park today with a good friend when I remarked that my beloved dog was eight and I was worried if I should get a puppy now to ease the pain I knew I would feel when Raffers went to dog heaven.

My friend leaned down, smiled, and whispered in Raffers' ear that I was thinking of getting a backup. It was his way of reminding me that the risks of love, because they are so great, don't come with a backup. Raff woofed and danced, unconcerned. The sun was out, and there were smells everywhere. He doesn't try to live ten years ahead; he's here now.

People who don't feel safe want control. Some people want control over everything, including grammar and their neighbor's lawn. They want an ordered world, and it makes them angry or frustrated when they cannot have it.

These people chop down trees so that not a branch extends into their view. They prefer a framed picture to a natural one. They will build a house that dominates a lot instead of caring about the harmony between land and building. They dream of more freeways A world with tight corners is a world separate from nature. It needs asphalt and concrete to exert control over plants, people, and animals. It is a world that for a moment seems safer with buildings instead of open space, and then suddenly feels colder and more ominous.

It is the difference between the diverse, somewhat messy plot that is Victor Steinbrueck Park at the Public Market in Seattle and the concrete and glass of Seattle's Westlake Center. They both have charms, but one is alive and the other is dead.

If you desire an edged lawn and an edged world, you will end up with an edged life. A tight, clean box is what you may want at the end of life, not throughout your life.

There is a balance possible between order and chaos. There is safety in a place that respects life in all its forms yet protects against the excesses of the elements that surround us.

When the light of spring draws you out of your house or car, be gentle in what you cut, build, move, and kill. You may not need all those edges. You may someday find you are happier without them.

The philosophers are always reminding us to "be here now." We should enjoy the process of life as much as the outcome. Whatever the activity, the finish is not the main source of joy.

When I became too busy to work in my garden I hired someone to do it for me. The garden looked beautiful but it wasn't mine anymore. I didn't know all the plants, I had not watched them emerge, I had not cared for them.

Now I am taking care of my garden again. I'm putting my spirit into the process instead of some idea of perfection. It doesn't look as controlled but it feels a lot better.

Whether it is parenting, building, writing, traveling, cleaning, or whatever you put your energy into, if you're not feeling the joy of the process, chances are you won't find the outcome more than a brief pleasure.

If you have enough money to hire your life out to others or too little time to take care of it yourself, you may lose it altogether. It's the difference between real intimacy versus the facade of a relationship, real flowers versus silk, living animals versus stuffed, and a life versus an appearance.

Vision Step Seven:
Commitment to Simplicity

Americans now joke about retail therapy. We go shopping in the hopes of acquiring just a little more safety but end up with just one more thing to store. We wake up tense on Saturday morning because we have so much stuff that needs new parts, or to be cleaned, or to be repaired. Somehow having is not being. The new technology that was to offer a life of ease has contributed to a life of speed and complexity. We are successful but we don't feel successful.

We are hungry for passion yet we fritter our lives away with details. We wear clothes that are not comfortable and that we cannot afford to have cleaned. We require perfection to make love, even though we know passion is messy. We design houses and yards we cannot relax in. We have so much, we move so fast, we cannot remember why we crossed the room.

A vision quest requires simplicity so that you are truly free to think and not do. Wisdom travels much slower and offers a much quieter beat than the lives many of us have chosen. Joseph Campbell reminds us that once the external is satisfied the values that produce joy are all within:

> People say that what we're all seeking is a meaning for life. I don't think that's what we're really seeking. I think that what we're seeking is an experience of being alive, so that our life experiences, on the purely physical plane, will have resonances within our own innermost being and reality, so that we actually feel the rapture of being alive.

Passion requires that you be unencumbered. Try to keep

all your arrangements as simple as possible. Take less with you rather than more, unless you need extra books, machines and clothing to feel safe. Bareness will drive you inward. If you have ever trekked with your complete survival needs on your back, then you know the pleasure of only carrying the essentials. It is a tremendous feeling of freedom and balance.

There is no need to suffer—that will distract you too. Be prepared and safe. Most of us do not want to spend much time in a tent or without shelter. A cabin in the wilderness or at the ocean, even a motel room, is fine as long as you can feel the environment and the solitude.

Simplicity limits the distractions of house, clothing, food, and equipment. Solitude reduces the other distractions. Try to clear your mind of things that you might use to divert yourself. Make a list of worries that pop into your mind so you can put them aside. Create temporary solutions for them so you will be less likely to be bothered by random thoughts.

Check on things you think you might have forgotten or that are nagging at you. Appoint a friend before you leave who will walk through your house, or anything that worries you, and check it out for you.

Relaxing is an art that few of us have mastered. There are many techniques to help you learn to let go. Use the ones that work for you. I find just creating a simple order with the few things I have brought with me works. It is like setting up an imaginary hut even if I am sitting on a beach. Do whatever you can to let go of the everyday until you are ready to stop fussing and relax.

The rapture of a vision is the meeting of the inner and outer worlds. When a single "happening" resonates, a path will begin to appear. It is a process of slowly becoming aware, becoming conscious of inner murmurings. A single event may not create a new vision, but many small steps will start the focus toward one.

Try to leave on your journey with the things of the small mind covered so you can allow the big mind space.

CHAPTER VIII

FEELINGS OF DEEP REST

We can make our minds so like still water that beings gather about us that they may see, it may be, their own images, and so live for a moment with a clearer, perhaps ever with a fiercer life because of our quiet.

—W. B. Yeats

If I had known what it would cost me to have it all, I would have settled for less.

—Lily Tomlin

Life is not getting what you want. It's wanting what you get.

—Tom Robbins

Stress is generated by internal events more frequently than by external events. It is not how much you do. It is the mind in relationship to what you do.

Twenty-three hundred years ago Aristotle concluded that, more than anything else, men and women seek happiness.

—Mihaly Csikszentmihalyi,
Flow: The Psychology of Optimal Experience

Flow is a powerful book. It is one of those rare texts that stretches your mind and clears your thoughts. It documents what we must know—that material goods, which we have increased a thousand times since Aristotle, will not provide happiness:

> Happiness is not something that happens. It is not the result of good fortune or random chance. It is not something that money can buy or power command.
>
> It does not depend on outside events but on how we interpret them. Happiness is a condition that must be prepared for, cultivated, and defended privately by each person. People who learn to control inner experience will be able to determine the quality of their lives, which is as close as any of us can come to being happy.

I have almost always been inordinately happy. Some have assumed it was because I did not know what was going on. Others knew I had faced an adverse childhood and painful life experiences and was keenly aware. I feel lucky and frequently, in my work, have asked the question Joseph Campbell asks, "Why do some people float in the waters that drown others?"

Csikszentmihalyi offers three answers:

- unself-conscious self-assurance—the implicit belief that your destiny is in your hands;

- focusing attention on the world—when attention is focused away from the self, frustrations of one's desires have less chance to disrupt consciousness;

- discovering new solutions—an open mind is prepared to perceive unexpected opportunities.

Pick up this book to lie on the grass with when the sun comes out or to curl up with on a rainy day. You deserve it.

I float my perfect flower in the perfect dish—and think of others perfecting their homes, clothing, bodies, and cars.

The aphid stumbling across my once-perfect flower tells me that none of us may ever own the ultimate.

There is only one Versailles, a year or two of the perfect body, a few thousand Ferraris.

Tomorrow we will seek another blossom, another car, a better body. We will try to duplicate, control, and own what we think are the best images.

Even if we assume we can have them, control them, keep them, what then? Wouldn't we move on?

Vision Step Eight:
Feelings of Deep Rest

We move so fast in American culture that few of us remember the feeling of deep rest. We are attracted to advertisements showing women who seem to be serenely napping in hot tubs or waking from a perfect night's sleep on a new mattress. We can rarely remember actually doing that ourselves. We may buy the hot tub or the mattress but not acquire the feelings of rest that attracted us in the first place.

Many of us are so out of touch with our bodies that we deny them the basic of rest. We pride ourselves on a discipline that gets more than it should out of us. Some of us see rest as wasted time instead of a source of energy and renewal.

Do you remember those special times on a vacation or when you have slept in and your mind and body feel just right? The body knows when it is ready to awaken if we do not override it with our demands. Deep rest occurs when you can set down the burdens of your day or life and feel the freedom of a new start. It is very hard to look at all that you carry unless you set it down.

Your mind cannot journey beyond the present without permission to do so. That permission comes when you allow it. When you commit to an opening and a releasing of the negative energy so the positive can surface.

There are many activities that help to eliminate distractions and achieve rest. Certain things create an experience of letting go in all of us. Some feel this way when swimming. They are creatures of the water and have always known it. Swimming laps or just being submerged in warm water gives them a feeling of deep rest. Exercise breaks down patterns of tension, and dancing, running, stretching, and aerobics work well.

Massage can be a wonderful source of deep rest because the laying on of hands is so healing. You are turning your body over to another person, whom you trust, to treat it gently and return it to you. Yoga can produce the same deep rest as therapeutic massage. Sitting quietly while you dream, staring into space, or emptying the mind can create a feeling of peace. It is a challenge to see how long you can sit with comfort and do nothing. Many of us have to learn to sit still, to relax, and let our minds clear or wander. That is why Americans pay for meditation classes. It does not seem to be a skill that we are allowed to grow up with.

Deep breathing is probably the most powerful source of a state of rest. The body needs air for life, but most of us breathe shallowly and quickly, whereas the lungs thrive on longer, deeper breaths.

I find sleep to be a wonderful restorer of spirit. Rearrange your schedule to allow enough sleep and a gentle awakening. Refuse to participate in activities that deny you rest. When time allows, let your body sleep as long as it wants to, undisturbed by light or sound. A vision journey requires the best of what you have physically, which is the body's most natural state.

CHAPTER IX

ELIMINATION OF DIVERSIONS

The work of preservation demands that the feelings playing about in one's guts not be turned into action. Just watch their passing like cherry blossoms.

—Maxine Hong Kingston,
Tripmaster Monkey

Gridlock stops our cars; gutlock stops our minds. Overstimulation can take away your joy. Cornering all that news in the newspapers, magazines, television, and radio is a high built on anxiety and pressure to keep up the pace.

Everything else is moving faster while we're gearing into overload.

Some of us run away to cabins or spas just to keep up. If you force yourself, daily, to balance constant information and competing and conflicting demands, you will reach the point where your mind will become disorganized. You will lose your ability to separate important from unimportant details.

Consider scanning and sorting so you can drop out the trivial, the irrelevant, and safeguard the essential. Try to eliminate the psychological buzz. Turn some of the information off. We are what we allow to flow through our brain.

Respect the art of being at peace.

Distraction is, always has been, and probably always will be, inherent in woman's life....The problem is not merely one of Woman and Career, Woman and the Home, Woman and Independence. It is more basically: how to remain whole in the midst of the distractions of life; how to remain balanced....

—Anne Morrow Lindbergh

Women's lives are usually broken up into more bits than men's. The birth of children stops and starts work and relationships. When we move to accommodate a spouse's career, it interrupts occupations and friendships. Taking care of aging parents changes plans and professional commitments.

We are always thinking of the whole of our lives—planning dinner while drafting a research project; talking to a colleague about company goals while thinking of the pain of a newly divorced friend. Life flows between sectors for us; it can rarely be controlled or compartmentalized. We weave and pile up bits to be squeezed into crevices of time.

Our lives are kaleidoscopes, boxes of puzzle pieces that make a whole. It works if you accept the creativity and the challenge of an improvised, unfinished quilt or the beauty of a wild garden. It works if you can hold on to the center of all the intertwining parts, the heart that turns many pieces into harmony.

The significant problems we face cannot be solved at the same level of thinking we were at when we created them.

—Albert Einstein

Many people on the fast track have begun to complain that their mind is wearing out. Do you worry about short-term memory loss? Does information sift out of your brain in seconds? Do you walk across a room and wonder on the other side what you wanted ? Do you forget the names of people you just met? Are you having new difficulty with spelling? Do you fear the early onset of Alzheimer's disease?

Let me reassure you your brain is most likely fine. What is happening is you have filled up your short-term memory chips. You are trying to remember four hundred times the information of a Renaissance man, let alone a Renaissance woman! You just don't have any more space. If you add in new information, other bits and pieces automatically drop out.

Your brain is full! The reason twenty-five-year-olds can remember things is because they still have empty space. With the daily explosion of information anyone past thirty has already stored far more than a traditional brain can remember.

Memory researchers will tell you that you can hold only three to seven items in your short-term memory at once. The range depends on your particular talents. If you try to hold more than seven thoughts you will lose most of them. Long-term memory is a little more solid because the acquisition process is slower and more controlled.

Just driving to work and listening to the radio will use up so much memory that you feel stressed out and grouchy. Sometimes you drive miles without being aware, you don't remember what you passed on the road. You wonder why you didn't run into something. Hopefully you have some sort of automatic pilot operating.

When you rode a horse instead of a car between home and

work it required less short-term memory. You were processing fewer images and signals. There was no radio to speed up audio messages and no technology to speed up responses.

You have essentially the same brain as you did on horse-back, just as you have the same hands. Until you develop ways to hold more short-term memory items—lists, notes, taping, delegating the information to someone else's memory, using the new technology of computer notebooks or mind-expanding and memory techniques—you will be frustrated and forgetful.

We have to update mind skills just as we update other skills. That is why so many people are encouraging you to set goals, have visions, know your priorities. Without these aids you will forget where you are going or why you wanted to go there.

Vision Step Nine:
Elimination of Diversions

Every bad feeling is potential energy toward a more right way of being if you give it space to move toward its rightness.

—Eugene Gendlin,
Focusing

It is time to resist all the diversions claiming your attention so there is room for something new. Settle yourself in all the ways you know will interfere with your concentration before you leave the known and predictable path. Clear a space for all of us.

Clearing the mind is very difficult in our complex world. We find it hard even to remember what we are worried about until our mind slows down. Making lists will help shore up your memory.

Carry a tablet or notebook around with you for a few days and write down everything that is worrying you. The list can include short-term, long-term, or future worries. Sit down and create a solution or a place to park each of these worries so they do not come up when you are working on deeper issues.

Sometimes a worry box works as a record. Put each worry on a card. List various solutions you have tried and the current one you are using. When a worry thought comes up see if you can make a note of it and put it back in the box. You can schedule times to review your worry cards instead of allowing them to pop into your head on impulse.

When you decide to take a vision journey, to create a time for understanding and change, put the worry box away as a symbol of release until you return. There will always be time to worry later. Start a list of needs for your time away and for anything you think might occur at home to interfere. Prepare for what you can. Ask a friend to check on your home, plants, and animals so you will feel at peace.

You can also make a comfort list of your friends, skills, resources, and alternatives. We are sometimes better at listing the negatives in our lives than we are the positives. Make a list of your assignments for the future as you now see them. It will be interesting to make a comparison when you have reviewed these assignments on a deeper level.

I always leave a clean house, laundry done, bills mailed, notes written, or calls made whenever I travel, regardless of the reason. I feel safer when I have ordered what I can order. External order seems to give permission for internal disorder.

One of the reasons many cultures insist that you leave home and seek a nonordinary reality for a vision quest is so that you can let go of everyday concerns. I have that feeling when I am flying in an airplane and looking out the window. My mind automatically drops the cares of the day and shifts to a higher plane. I begin to think about the meaning of my life, my values, and I settle into a gentle philosophical time.

You will begin to feel the release from diversions once you start the trip away. Removal from the noise and speed of everyday life by traveling to a remote or at least a quieter place always helps. The environment has tremendous power. Go to where you are most deeply touched by nature.

Choose a place that allows you to let go of the "buzz" inside you because it provides no noise and no reinforcement. Without cars, telephones, media, crowds, and obligations, you will slow down automatically. You will begin to catch up with yourself and begin to find answers to your questions.

Wisdom travels at one mile an hour; it cannot catch you if you are still traveling at sixty miles an hour. Try to match the pace of wisdom.

CHAPTER X

BALANCING RITUALS

Breath is the bridge which connects life to consciousness, which unites your body to your thoughts. Whenever your mind becomes scattered, use your breath as the means to take hold of your mind again.

—Thich Nhat Hanh,
The Miracle of Mindfulness

Connect yourself to each season. August is a wonderful time in the Northwest. It's a time to step outside and offer a moment of appreciation. It's a time to organize your own awards ceremony for achieving balance.

The monarch butterfly deserves recognition for persistence in spite of multiple dangers. A bow as they flutter by will do.

The songbird award to all those tiny beings that sing away despite the competition from cars, lawn mowers, and aircraft.

The "still smells good" award to the roses, newly cut grass, and salt water.

The commitment award to all the insects that go about their business no matter what. I have ants in my mailbox and bees in my birdhouse. I applaud their ability to adapt.

Take a walk around your yard and neighborhood and offer recognition to anyone and anything that merits reinforcement for a job well done.

On your return award yourself the "quality of life medal" because you live fully and with love in a complex, ever-changing world.

There will always be pain in our lives: The pain of not understanding. The pain of missed dreams. The pain of broken relationships.

There are alternatives to pain. We can smother it with being busy, with work, alcohol, other drugs, and repression. We can abuse others with it. We can abuse ourselves.

Or we can do our homework, understand the mechanism of the trap we are caught in, and learn enough to spring it.

Albert Einstein said that we often suffer from a sort of optical delusion. We act as if we are not connected to everything and everybody. We think we can separate ourselves from people who are different. We think that we are not connected to life in all its forms. It is the most painful delusion in the world today.

Vision Step Ten:
Balancing Rituals

Many wisdom traditions recognize how hard it is to clear the mind, so they use special rituals. Spinning prayer wheels, rosaries, chanting, singing, dancing, Tai Chi—all concentrate the mind on the clear space. Church ceremonies, making circles of stone, the beautiful Hopi and Tibetan sand paintings are all rituals of both respect and concentration.

The smell of incense immediately takes me to church, even if my eyes are closed. I was raised in one of those small, dark, mysterious-with-stained-glass Anglican churches. Any of the senses responds strongly to memory, and just triggering one of them can put you into the right frame of mind. Hymns resonate in the hearts of many of us. Candles are powerful symbols in some cultures.

Any symbol that centers the mind is useful. Wisdom traditions create a certain set of ritual movements or objects to speed up memory and return us to a place in our mind where all things become clarified and balanced. Hypnosis is a relaxation technique that can free the mind to remember or concentrate. Many of the exercises that create physical balance and simplicity also balance the mind.

These circumstances are called rites of intensification by anthropologists and are part of many vision quests. Some of these rites involve the whole group or community instead of you alone. Societies may hold rites of intensification to protect a village; to ensure rain, sun, or fertility; or to prepare the way for an individual undertaking a vision journey.

You may decide to hold a celebration for your friends and family before you start on a new "way" or a vision journey. The power of our human resources surrounding us and offering their help is not to be underestimated.

Thanksgiving is an example of a feast, a celebration of the harvest that can be seen as an intensification ritual. The table laden with food allays the fears of those who remember hard winters and less successful harvests. It is an accounting of the resources for the season ahead.

There are as many balancing rituals as there are communities. It is the unique nature of humans to keep inventing new ways to live and to experience. Some American snake handlers believe that picking up a large, venomous rattlesnake is a confrontation with the supernatural. Those free of sin will be cleansed. Those who are not free of sin will be bitten and die.

These tests seem bizarre until you imagine the blind scales of justice and all the ways throughout history we have used to keep them balanced. Accused persons used to be held underwater under the belief that the innocent would not drown but would somehow be rescued by God.

I was raised to believe that the symbolic consumption of the body and blood of Christ would restore my spirit. Confession and absolution are common rituals in all religions. Religious phenomena of all sorts, including bones, robes, and other relics, have always been used to evoke powerful emotional responses.

Each of us has our own sense of what creates balance within. Some of you just list your concerns, the positives and negatives, a life review, and then send it up the chimney. Jigsaw puzzles and gardening are wonderful concentration tools for me. Bonsai gardening or the tea ceremony extends a ritual one step farther. What clears your mind and brings you to your center? You know the feeling of balance. What do you have to do now to achieve it?

CHAPTER XI

ACCEPTANCE OF HUMILITY

Why doesn't anyone see God anymore?
Because no one can bend low enough.

—Robert Bly

I imagine one of the reasons people cling to their hates so stubbornly is because they sense, once hate is gone, they will be forced to deal with pain.

—James Baldwin,
in *James Baldwin: Artist on Fire*,
by W. J. Weatherby

And then, not expecting it, you become middle-aged and anonymous. No one notices you. You achieve a wonderful freedom. It is a positive thing. You can move about, unnoticed and invisible.

—Doris Lessing

Regrets, we all have a few. There is a little pang of grief at what might have been. But each regret is only a tender reminder of the wonder that is the present. The event that created the regret was somehow necessary.

Welcome those vulnerable messengers from the past as reminders of all the roads that led you here.

Vision Step Eleven:
Acceptance of Humility

The most beautiful and most profound emotion we can experience is the sensation of the mystical. It is the sower of the true science. He to whom this emotion is a stranger—who can no longer stand wrapped in awe—is as good as dead. That deeply emotional conviction of the presence of a superior reasoning power which is revealed in the incomprehensible universe forms my idea of God.

—Albert Einstein

Access to wisdom, to the resources of a greater power, requires that we recognize the limits of our own. The "spirits" will be with you only if you treat them with respect. Connections to a nonordinary reality, to the power of the supernatural, assumes you accept the existence of a power greater than human.

Each of us goes on a vision quest in a condition of poverty and need. We abandon, albeit briefly, the protection of material goods and structure. Tribes often created ego poverty through fasting, self-flagellation, self-mutilation, and prostration. Many Christian sects believe you must approach God with your eyes cast down, on your knees, covered in sackcloth and ashes.

Suffering is thought to produce a heightened state of awareness. The ordeals of a quest were believed to allow the breakthrough to special knowledge and the revealing of the sacred. We do not need to create such physical suffering. We can be humble. We can open our hearts, minds, and souls in other ways.

Sacrifice is also believed to be a ritual of humility. The willingness to make a present to the supernatural power is a recognition of your own inferior position as a supplicant. Suffering is a form of sacrifice, but many cultures believe that the giving up of time, ego, or property is just as powerful. Given our current life-style and values, time may be a most appropriate sacrifice.

Humility is not fear. Long ago we assumed the gods were hostile because there were so many unknowns in the environment. We felt they wanted to see our pain to be reassured we were less than they and would not challenge them. Many religious traditions were based on fear and placation, the idea of sacrifice carried to extremes. Later in history many Christians, through the New Testament, transferred their beliefs to a compassionate, loving God.

Now we are less afraid and free to recognize and feel that the natural powers are positive. Johann Goethe believed that when the individual makes a sincere commitment, the universe moves to assist him. I know it does. There is an almost instant response. You must open to be able to feel it.

Many of the Northwest Coast tribes understood the process of opening. They required a private but complete confession of all the faults of living the supplicant had committed. Their rituals of humility are not very different from the confession and purification rituals of the Catholic Church. The church requires you, on your knees, to ask for help and forgiveness while listing your sins. You must then do a penance.

Try to clear out the recent past by recognizing personal mistakes and errors. List those circumstances where you were unkind, not gentle, disrespectful of life. Think about ways to release the negative energy. Assign an appropriate penance that is productive.

Make your apologies in whatever way you can. Plan to atone. Create balance between yourself and the universe. Forgive yourself and others, and nature will receive you.

When you have looked within yourself and cleared a space, you can begin to concentrate intensely. Heightened awareness, with minimal thought to self, assists in the interpretation of impressions and the understanding of the subtleties inherent in this journey.

The heart of humility that is always a part of requests made to greater powers is the understanding that even our most personal visions must have value for the community and the earth. You are not seeking answers only to your questions, but so that you can give more to those around you. All wisdom traditions state clearly that a vision is invalid if it is not for the greater good of the community. It must have significance for the planet.

The frame of your mind is the most important condition of this journey. The clarity and effects of a vision are thought to be in proportion to the sincerity of the seeker.

CHAPTER XII

STATE OF VULNERABILITY

The soul does not like unconscious ecstasy.

—Robert Bly

One of the pains of childhood is that no matter how much attention we get now, it is never the same as having them clap then.

A moment of respect and honor for all of you, the personal astronauts hurtling about in the inner cosmos. You are pioneers climbing new mountains, sliding into ravines with no map except faith. You have no safety cord. You have let go of the limits of the past and are unwilling to settle for security. You want something deeper.

My love goes out to you for the pain you feel, for the wisdom you share with the rest of us. Thank you for the maps you will one day provide—paths cleared by your tears and kept open by the honesty of your heart.

A Father's Day offering, letter of understanding:

Dear Dad:

I was not what you had dreamed of and you were not a good parent. It has taken me forty years to understand you did the best you could with who you were and what you knew. You were a man of passion and violence. I've kept the passion. You were a man of humor and melancholy. I've kept the humor. You had strong prejudices and generations of anger. I'll let them go. You cared about your community, your country, and your honor. I've kept these lessons deep within. Today is a day to remember the gifts you gave to me, the love you felt, though rarely expressed. Today is the day to let the generations of pain drift away forever, by understanding, acceptance, and time.

I'm laying this letter on your grave to put the spirit between us to rest. It is possible now to love each other fully, no regrets, only the chance to take the best of both of us into the future.

Your daughter,

Jennifer

There is no pain quite like that of a broken heart. The experience of loss in love wounds us like no other. In the midst of our pain, we cry out, wishing there was something to take the hurt away. But there is nothing. There is no cure for a broken heart except for that universal healer, time.

If there is no cure for a broken heart, neither is there a guaranteed way to avoid having one. The more you risk, the more people you grow to love, the more it is possible that you will experience a separation. Yet whenever your heart is broken, you receive a blessing; your broken heart becomes an open heart.

When we experience sadness and grief, something unexpected emerges.

When we allow ourselves to be broken, a gentle transformation takes place. In the midst of the pain, we feel a softness and a vulnerability that are truly beautiful. We become more accepting and open. Judgment and criticism are replaced by a compassion for others and an acceptance of life the way it is.

—Douglas Bloch,
Words That Heal

Vision Step Twelve:
State of Vulnerability

With humility comes vulnerability. We admit our ignorance and our weakness. In the Christian traditions I believe
that the prophecy "But the meek shall inherit the earth and
delight themselves in the abundance of peace" (Psalms 37:11)
refers not to a demeanor with one's fellow humans as much as
a willingness to be vulnerable before both a greater power and
the wonders of the world.

"Inherit" means not the riches of the material life but the
richness of deep awareness. The world becomes ours because
we can feel it, smell it, touch it, and love it. Heaven on earth.
Heaven is this reality and our oneness with it. Ashes to ashes,
dust to dust. There is no need for an afterlife if one is life.

Reception to the divine is based on an openness to all reali-
ties. This was a natural part of the spiritual way of many cultures. It is somehow not natural for us. We have been raised to
defend ourselves against supernatural experiences and the environment. We have given more weight to logic than intuition, to
ego rather than community, to Christianity than to nature. We
have been afraid.

The power is always there. The key lies in one's ability to
apprehend it, to be ready, to feel safe with it. The success and
effect of a vision experience are in direct proportion to the
availability of the seeker. You must be willing to allow your
heart and mind to be touched. We are each called, on this
path, to be our own unique self. Only then can we see and
support others. The validation of self is a key vision experience.

We have always had a desire, a remarkable need to transcend
ourselves, and now we are far more able to do so. Skills that were

once available only to "specialists" are now available to all of us. Time and opportunity have been given to us.

We are now far safer in our bodies and minds. We are more at home in our psyches. We do not need to spend a lifetime experimenting to be able to converse with ourselves. We have been raised in a psychological age that creates a foundation again for a step into the spiritual and natural realms.

Those who traveled long before us accepted the power of nature but rarely their own power. Opening to the unconscious was once discouraged as sin. It was repressed except in the form of dreams. Dreams were thought to be the language of gods or spirits.

We now have far more access to unconscious information and cultural permission to be adventurous with feelings. We do not need to hide so much from ourselves and others. We can feel our own power and the power of the universe. We can understand our dreams in a more personal sense.

In many tribes a spiritual leader will take you up to this point of preparation and then leave you alone to carry out your mission. You can instead find a vision quest guide, join a class, or go with a group that prepares and supervises people on vision journeys. You must decide yourself, at this point, whether you need the additional support and information of someone with experience.

Openness, in every way, is the assignment at this step on the path. Openness allows attention to sensory experience, the silences and sounds of the environment. Your vulnerability, your sensitivity is the softness that makes you available to wisdom.

CHAPTER XIII

CLARIFYING THE MISSION

The great malady of the twentieth century, implicated in all our troubles and affecting us individually and socially, is loss of soul. When the soul is neglected, it doesn't just go away; it appears in obsessions, addictions, violence, and loss of meaning. If the soul's capacity for creativity is not honored it will wreak havoc instead.

No age has been exempt from the loss of soul, but this century's loss is compounded further by our ignorance of what the soul is. The soul has been waxed and polished by theologians into oblivion. It is impossible to define but I think of it as a kind of force that grazes where it will, always striving to connect more firmly to life.

—paraphrased from *A Guide for Cultivating Depth and Sacredness in Everyday Life,* by Thomas More

*To cheat oneself out of love is the most terrible decep-
tion; it is an eternal loss for which there is no repara-
tion, either in time or in eternity.*
—Søren Kierkegaard

Sigmund Freud said that there is work and there is love. That is what life is. Make sure you have the time and energy for both.

A friend and I were walking on one of these wonderful summer evenings, trying to define success. She was moving to a smaller house, a symbolic drop in her standard of living, and she wondered if it meant she was less successful.

It seems so much harder to define success than in decades past, when society and money were more obvious criteria. Some of our peers had big houses and gave big parties. We didn't even like big parties. Were we odd, or just envious? Success has become so much more individual.

We tried a review of possible measures of success. We passed the children test; they were fine except for their potential to turn out more conservative than we were. We liked our mothers and our friends.

We failed the marriage test. We knew people celebrating twenty-five years, and we were unlikely to accomplish that. Yet we were happier with the love in our lives than we ever had been before.

The professional test was ambivalent. We had given up regular, respected careers for independence. We were free-lancers with few standard measures of merit. We passed the health test, the stress test, and the clean-house test.

It became obvious why we had become such good friends, but what was the one thing that would define a life as a contribution? We both knew we could do much more for our communities.

Money, goods, style, and status did not connect deeply with us, but we finally realized kindness did. Success was simple—it was the absence of meanness.

Meanness in otherwise successful people had always stunned us because it was so unexpected. Meanness, in all its forms, breaks trust in self, others, and humanity.

We were okay. We had mean thoughts, but we had always struggled to be kind. That was a worthwhile measure of success on a summer evening in Seattle.

The next subject was ice cream. We both had chocolate.

Many of us find it easier to love than to be loved. Long-held patterns of rejection and abandonment limit our belief in our own value.

We resist the efforts of others to love us and sometimes we extinguish that love. The more you accept, the less there is to resist.

Love requires the willingness to be loved.

Vision Step Thirteen:
Clarifying the Mission

You may have had a known mission when you decided to start this journey. Illness, divorce, unemployment, loss, or change can clarify our priorities very quickly. You may want a deeper understanding of why you are alone, what happened to the relationship, or just help!

There are so many questions in life that we have to set priorities.

Often answering the big ones settles the little ones. What do you want to know about yourself? What do you want to understand about the world you live in? What do you need to know about your work or your future? Why do you want to know or understand? Motivation is a key to truth. You must know your motivation, it must be positive, before you have a chance of success in your mission.

Many of us do not even have specific questions or problems to solve. Our questions might be: What is this about me? Am I okay? What is missing? Is anything missing? How am I at this moment in time? What do I want? What is truly important to me? What do I want to be able to believe about myself? Where am I going? What can I know about myself? Where do you want to go? What is entering your life at this time? What is leaving your life?

A general life review is always valuable. Most cultures believe it should be a regular (every seven to ten years) assignment. I think we should do at least a mini-review every week, on a day we respect as holy.

There are many questions so choose ones that fit you, that resonate or seem to touch you. When the mission is general, there are known criteria for creating a personal vision:

- Identify the quality of life you really want.

- Imagine yourself achieving it. What does it look and feel like?

- Identify the strategies that will lead to your success.

- Recognize and list the barriers to what you want.

- Develop a workable bridge and support system between today and your future.

- Create an alignment of attitudes, beliefs, and values to enable you to take the next step.

A vision plan will reveal the information you need to move into your own future and increase the quality of your life and the lives of those around you. In this sense it is a clarifier and an energizer for what you know you want.

The unknown, or a more specific mission, can be harder than a life review but consequently more rewarding. When you ask, "What is it about me?" you may get an answer that hurts or startles. When you ask, "What happened to my marriage?" you may find out that you were not willing to be intimate, that you were not truly available for marriage.

The most important vision journey I took had as its mission the question "What is this hole in your center, this missing part, that keeps you somehow detached from people?" It had taken me so long to realize it was there because I was so skilled at covering it up. I selected relationships that would not challenge the flaw.

A divorce finally forced me to ask this question on the deepest level of my being and not to give up until an answer resonated within me. This quest of mine was both general, What is going on? and specific, What has kept me cut off from intimacy?

The process of clarifying your mission can be very powerful. It is powerful because it represents and communicates one's purpose: "Here is what I stand for; here is what I believe; here is what I am committed to."

It inspires people to reach for what could be in their lives. People who create personal visions rise above their fears and preoccupations with current reality. They embrace their highest values and aspirations. They take the hero's path.

CHAPTER XIV

~

CHOOSING THE WAY

The task is to go deeply as possible into the darkness, to name the pain that one finds there, and the truth of one's perceptions, and to emerge on the other side with permission to name one's reality from one's own point of view.

—Anthea Francine,
Envising Theology

I feel like I am on a long train ride. At the moment the train is rounding, at a very slow speed, a big curve in the tracks. At the beginning of the curve Chad got off the train. I know that this is not a return-trip ride. I am helpless in looking back, always looking back as my ride goes on. I know I cannot get off and run back to get Chad. The train chugs on and all I can do is look longingly back, back to that part of the journey when Chad rode with me, with Marilyn and with Stacey. It was a wonderful journey.

It was the best part of my ride through life.

Until this train stops to let me off I will never be far from Chad's life. I could never be.

—Art Martinson,
Chad's father

Art is a friend of mine. He is a gentle man, happiest when hiking a trail in the wilderness. His seventeen-year-old son was killed last September by a drunk driver.

114

I am out here looking over the incredibly old, rocky coast of South Wales. Looking for a missing part of me, trying to link up.

This may be the pain of all immigrants trying to find a touchstone because they have lost their history. We wander around moors and ancient cities trying to connect to our roots.

Those who never left their beginnings can feel the safety of knowledge and ways that go back ten centuries, as familiar as the breath of their life.

When you disconnect, it stays with you forever. You are like a refugee who remembers smells, sounds, tastes, climate, and flowers he will never know again.

Some do not feel the need to look back, but most do. We want to feel complete, to reconcile within us the disparate parts.

All of us can find peace taking journeys backward, understanding and laying to rest the spirits of the past, learning the other landscapes that connect us to the Earth and are so much a part of what we are.

Once you have laid the spirits of other worlds to rest, you can more easily re-create your own world.

I had the good fortune one week to attend a workshop with Robert Bly and Marion Woodman. They are two of the most original and powerful writers on this decade's questions about masculine and feminine. The seminar was a fascinating combination of poetry, mythology, and analysis. One of the stories was a Native American myth

> We knew that the white man was coming. We knew he would want to take everything. We met to try to decide where we could hide the most valuable of our treasures. We asked each other, Where will the treasures be safe?
>
> One chief suggested we hide our goods in caves, but another said, "No, the white men are like ants, they swarm everywhere, they will enter all the caves." Another chief thought we could put them under the water of the rivers. "That won't work," someone said, "They fish, they will scrape the bottoms of our rivers and take everything."
>
> Finally they decided to hide their treasures in the white man's heart. "He will never look there."

It is hard to be part of such a story. Our pride requires a rethinking of intentions and how they may have changed over time. Most of us need teachers to help us repair love in this world. Bly and Woodman are master teachers. They say the answers lie in the shadows.

Robert Bly suggested that when we are angry we imagine who we hate, glare at them, break eye contact, look down quickly to the left, and we will see our own shadow.

Vision Step Fourteen:
Choosing the Way

Once you have chosen your mission, it is time to consider the way. Do you want to take a path through to the light or the dark sources of information?

Most religions or spiritual journeys seem to emphasize light. Sunrise services, candles, crystals, arms stretched upward as the spires of churches take us closer to heaven. The word "light" is a word of impact, of opening. The idea of breaking through to the light, becoming light, feeling the light within. It is an outward journey to create a oneness with the universe. It requires no special instructions beyond those in the other vision steps. It is a familiar path.

There are many paths to the center. Some emphasize the dark. These are the vision journeys that move deeper within you. Many cultures believe you must pass through the dark to reach the light. There is a resistance to the dark side, or it is thought best left to the therapists to delve into the painful side of our ego. You make the choice.

The shadow is a very old theme in mythology and religion. Heroes had to travel through hell and confront monsters to reach heaven or love. The Crucifixion is a horrible death leading to eternal life. The path of the martyr was usually one of torture. When hallucinogenic drugs were used to seek enlightenment, many people felt they lost control when visions opened before them. They panicked and ended up on "bad trips." They were seeking pleasure and rejected the information their mind presented. Tribes that used mind-altering drugs, like peyote, sought understanding, not isolated sensations. They expected intense experiences. Without preparation the conflict between light and dark can seem like madness.

Shamanic journeys always seek the dark path to find understanding and vision. They do not require drugs, just deep relaxation or intensification. Drums or chants are often an important part of the journey inward. It is an image of going deep into the earth (or self), instead of upward and away from the earth. It is a heavier, more fearsome image, and its power is great.

A shamanic journey is less familiar in American culture. You will need to do more reading in this area before actually attempting a shadow journey. These are the basic steps:

Put yourself in a darkened place, either outside at night, in a building or in a tent that light does not penetrate, or cover your eyes in some way.

Find within your mind an image of a hole in the earth through which you can gain the illusion of access. It should be an actual hole in the environment (cave, crevasse, hollow tree, gopher hole, well) into which you can let your mind wander. Remember *Alice In Wonderland*.

At some point on your journey downward, through this hole that you can visualize, look for a tunnel. There may be many tunnels, or it may just seem like a big black space. There should be a feeling of heading downward until you feel you have come out the other side into what shamans call "the lower world."

Ed Gross, in his audiotape *Course in Shamanism*, suggests you return at this point to the surface, with nothing changed within you, as a form of practice. You need to feel comfortable with your ability to come and go when traveling in unfamiliar psychic territory.

When you feel rested and ready, use your mind to return into the earth and ask for an animal escort (mammal or bird). It must be a wild animal, because domesticated animals have lost their power. It cannot be a reptile, because they are not warm-blooded. An image of an animal or bird will appear. It may be a bear, eagle, rat, or lion—all animals and birds have some unique power. My spirit came in the form of an owl.

This animal becomes your totem or protector, and in many tribes was a lifetime source of power that might be incorporated into your name. The human/animal alliance recognizes the oneness of life forms. You probably have an affinity for an animal or bird now but have not seen it as a guide.

At this point you can begin your mission, begin to ask your questions and ask the animal to help. It may take more than one animal in your consciousness to find an answer. Some animals will have power and therefore information for you; others may not. Any animal that seems threatening is to be avoided; gently pass by.

Many shamans report the feeling of encountering in the darkness a bridge that they must cross with the help of their "power animal" before they can hear what the universe is trying to tell them. It is a further bridge into "sacred space" or nonordinary reality. When you feel uncomfortable, always return to the surface.

Psychotherapy or counseling, in almost any form, can also be a journey into the dark side. We haven't traditionally referred to "analysis" as a vision quest because we have pretended it is a rational process grounded in acceptable reality.

Anyone who has participated in the process as either healer or client knows the truth of the peeling away of the layers of our behavior and understanding. The journey to "true self" is a vision quest of the most intimate kind. It is a way of passing through the dark, the tunnel, into the light of personal acceptance.

You can choose either way, but in your lifetime there will be journeys filled with light and those that take you to darker realms within nature and your own mind. The light and the dark are equal in their power, goodness, and visionary capacity.

Consider your questions and their connection to you. Is this to be an external or an internal journey? This is highly personal territory. Let your sense of self and your sense of safety guide you.

CHAPTER XV

FINDING THE SENSE

The silence that reveals its own truth.

—T. S. Eliot

Creativity is a crucial element of the passionate life. The Greeks called it a divine power. Yet it's like a sense of humor; if you don't have it, how can you get it?

> *Imagination is the beginning of creation. You imagine what you desire, you will what you imagine, and at last you create what you will.*
> —George Bernard Shaw

> *When something needs to be painted it lets me know.*
>
> —Luis Frangella

> *The way to get good ideas is to get lots of ideas and throw the bad ones away.*
> —Linus Pauling

Creativity seems to thrive on confusion and disorder. It is the randomness we will allow in our mind and life that produces strange and wonderful thoughts.

Sometimes the incubation phase of a new possibility feels like neutral, blank, until the elements combine. Accepting the muddle, letting go, allows old elements to emerge in new forms.

So put up your feet, take a deep breath, give in to some random thoughts and feelings. Tell anyone who purses his lips or wrinkles his brow to relax. You're working hard creating the future.

Disappointments touch every life. They are usually connected to the creation of expectations instead of the acceptance of the process that is life. When we create a need for a certain outcome, we forget the pleasure of the journey. Life has more joy if you can:

- Foresee a variety of outcomes to any experience.

- Accept change in everything.

- Try to be realistic about what makes a good life.

- Expect some disappointments.

- Take care of yourself every day.

- Look for an average that is good, not a high expectation for every event and every person.

Seeing only one way to happiness, "tunnel-vision thinking," sets you up for loss. Happiness is not a single person, job, or event, it is a life.

Robert Bly has an unpublished poem about the bird skeletons he used to find in old barns. He wondered why they were there. Little birds had somehow gotten trapped when the barn was cleaned out and closed.

He imagined that they kept flying up toward the window at the top of the barn, battering themselves against the light, until they starved or died of thirst.

The only way out was the dark holes the rats come through. Birds do not see the floor as opportunity.

Sometimes the answers are on the floor.

It starts early, so much earlier than any of us want to believe. You cannot remember but it is there, the sense of missing pieces. You know there are bits of yourself that you have lost and if you could reconnect them all you would be stronger, smarter, happier. The puzzle that is you is incomplete, parts lost in utero, at birth, in childhood, through life experience.

It is this incompleteness that makes us resist intimacy and joy. The missing pieces limit our ability to feel, to understand, to contribute. The lost pieces limit our willingness to give to others. We hold on too tightly to ours and it never becomes yours. We are waiting for a sense of our own completion before we will provide pieces for others.

Resist the temptation to say "not me," because it is you, whether you can dismiss these ideas or not. There are degrees of attachment; some of you have less you long for than others. Some of you are hungrier than others. Regardless, the desire to be complete is unsuppressible and endless.

The puzzle pieces are all there in your memory, in the cells of your body. You can feel them, smell them, sometimes even catch a glimpse of them like a flash of light, but they will not come to you. You must open up, trust yourself, and take the time to conduct the search. There are many who will help you, or it can, with commitment, be done alone.

It is an assignment for the next century. We need to expand our hearts and minds to match the requirements of a global community. Your body is changing, your life span is extending, your personality must stretch to accommodate the future. You need all the pieces to be unbroken. If you will work, at the deepest levels, to create harmony in your own life, you will be able to contribute to the harmony of the world.

Vision Step Fifteen:
*Finding the Feeling**

Whatever way you choose to put yourself in a closer balance with yourself and your environment, you will be flooded with information. Your choice of subjects to explore may surprise you. Intuitive wisdom will bring up the heart of a problem when our mundane self may be concentrating on something entirely different that is only a symptom of deeper issues.

Now is the point at which you review your agenda. Turn deep within when you are at a place of calm and deep rest and ask yourself about the quality of your life. How does it feel? What is most important to you at this moment in time? What has brought you to this place? What do you want to know? If there are too many questions, let them revolve around in your mind and body freely until one or two take precedence and seem to carry more power and emotion. You have all the time you need to sort.

It may help to center on a particular area of your life: family, self, professional, community, health, relationship, etc. If no questions appear or none seems particularly intense, just relax, breathe, and feel your body. A lack of information is almost always due to a block or tension within the body. When the body releases, the mind does.

Be gentle with yourself, take very small steps with the play of emotions until you make a visceral connection. If you are stuck, Eugene Gendlin, in his book *Focusing,* offers physical ways to tap into the sense of what you may now be feeling or

---

*Note: Eugene Gendlin, in his book *Focusing,* introduced some of the ideas in this section.

126

trying to formulate into a question. His exercises are designed to help you get in better touch with your body.

Choose one idea from those you are considering. How does the question or problem feel? Can you get a "felt sense" of it in your body? Is there a tingle or a "hit" of recognition that this has power for you? Do tears begin to flow, or do you feel pleasure? Are you afraid, or is there anticipation?

Most questions or thoughts have more than one element to them. One way to clarify a problem is to break it into parts and think about them one at a time.

Try at this point to name what you are feeling. Try to name the emotion until there is a fit. Test the fit until it feels right. Does your question, feeling, or problem make you confused, tense, heavy, tired, excited, open, closed, etc.? What seems to be the worst part of it? What is the best? Can you give it a name and formulate a question?

Can you describe it? Is it big, little, light, dark, old, new? Your body knows, and it will tell you. As you experience these feelings or remember something that happened to you, are you younger, a child, your present age, older, or scared?

Once you know the feeling, ask, What would expand this feeling? What would change this feeling? How would I feel if I understood this problem or it was completely resolved? You need to know the quality and intensity of what you are trying to ask.

I had resolved to ask about the feeling that something was missing inside of me. It had led to unreasonable fear on more than one occasion. It was strongest whenever I tried to love and trust someone. I thought that this question contained my deepest secrets.

Say out loud the word or words that come closest to describing what you feel, or write them down. Do they resonate within you? Often you will feel your stomach jump with a little spasm of pleasure when the link is made. Your body and mind are so pleased to be connected again. Any bodily signals, especially sexual ones, will affirm the power and the importance of your question. A body "shift" of any kind is the beginning of a transformation.

Receive whatever comes with an open heart; stay vulnerable. Sift information rather than quickly grabbing it. Gently clarify what you feel, and see if it is possible to put it into words.

Let the sense move around in your body until you can name it. The name that eventually resonated deeply within my heart was "abandonment." It was the word that turned up after "bad," "empty," "thin," "lost," "young," "dark," "old," "closed," "hole," "too late," "alone," "unloved," "unlovable," "afraid."

You may ask questions over days or hours and you may receive answers in the same way. It is important to keep your heart open, to move slowly, to maintain your solitude, to be gentle with yourself until you feel the quest, for this moment in time, is complete. It will be obvious when it is finished. You will feel clear, energized, or you may just want to curl up and go to sleep.

CHAPTER XVI

ASKING AND RECEIVING

We must learn to hear the tongue of the Invisible.

—Koran

When we are young and someone attacks us, we don't ask many questions. We are surprised and hurt. I call it the Easter Bunny theory of life: "If I am good, everyone will be good to me."

When we grow up, the questions about personal attacks start. We begin to separate ourselves from our circumstances. We learn that we are old enough to protect ourselves. We can no longer pretend to be surprised, unaware of others and reality. We have to give up the illusions that everyone means well.

Let go of the role of victim, grow up, accept life and people. Take good care of yourself. Trade innocence and illusion for awareness and grace.

Here we are opening into "the religion of psychology" by suggesting that psychology is a variety of religious experience....Psychology as religion implies imagining all psychological events as effects of Gods in the soul, and all activities to do with soul, such as therapy, to be operations of ritual in relation to these Gods....It is not a question of religion turning to psychology—no, psychology is simply going home.

— James Hillman,
Re-Visioning Psychology

We are so good at concealing our feelings and not making demands on those we love. Yet, it hurts so much more when we don't tell the truth. It makes your body ache with anxiety, the mixed messages confuse the other person, your relationship gets crazy. People are intuitive, they know when things are unclear. They cannot truly be fooled. When you know, let them know.

Tell the truth quickly.

If we can contain the conflict of the opposites—what our small egos want as opposed to what the Self or Destiny has ordained—if we can hold at the center, then we learn to think with the heart. We can know what we feel, know what we desire, and at the same time gradually surrender to our larger circumference. Then without becoming bitter or cutting ourselves off from our own reality, we can consciously accept what is happening. Aware of both sides, the mind can accept what is happening. Aware of both sides, the mind can accept and the heart can continue to feel. Where mind and heart are tearing apart, thinking with the heart is the only way to transcend the opposites. What would otherwise be the salt of bitterness can thus become the salt of wisdom.

—Marion Woodman,
The Pregnant Virgin

Vision Step Sixteen:
Asking and Receiving

The core of a vision journey is the process of asking for information from the sources around you and being able to receive the answers. When you have found comfort with a way to reach deeper within, choose just one of the feeling words you have discovered or one of the questions that has power for you. Reconsider it, try to flow through it and around it, and then stand back from it. Imagine yourself as a spirit actually flying into the center of the feeling or question. What do you find? Ask for help from the natural resources around you.

If you are unable to form your thoughts into a question or word, then just ask again, "What is this feeling? What does it mean for me, for my life?" You will get many answers or only one. If you get many, some will be transitory and will produce no further visceral shift within you. Let them go by until you receive an answer or information that produces a sense you can feel.

Each answer that fits will create a little or a big "wow" deep within. You will know. It is like an orgasm; there is no confusion when one has occurred. Receive whatever comes with an open heart; stay vulnerable.

Consider the information that continues to flood your mind and body rather than quickly accepting it. Probe the answers, check the feel, and repeat your questions. Try again to gently clarify what you feel and see if it is possible to put it into words. If you have decided to keep a journal, now may be the time to write down what you have known.

You may continue to ask questions. It is important to keep your mind open, to maintain your solitude, until you are tired. It will be obvious when you are finished. You will find yourself slipping into neutral, wanting to walk or putter around while your mind and body process all you have felt and learned.

When I first took these steps, I had a very open agenda. What was this feeling inside that seemed to limit me in so many ways? I asked the question. The feelings around it were fear and pain. Eventually when the a word "abandonment" formed out of these, I knew I had a handle on the barrier in my life. It was a fit deep within me. I knew it was the truth.

Information came flooding in. As a small child, almost from birth, I had been left. I was born in London during World War II. My parents were both police officers, and their duties during the war and the bombings took them away. My brother and I were sent out of the city, as many children were, to the safety of the countryside. I was moved often from relatives to foster homes to orphanages and to places my parents were assigned.

When my father was sent back to work in the mines for three months to produce coal for the war effort, I went with him and was put into day care. I was only two, but memories were so powerful I could even smell those around me. I knew then that as a very small child I had been abused in some way. I could smell the person who had hurt me.

I had sought that smell out my whole life and never known why. Somehow that hurt, whatever it was, sent me so far inside myself that only as a mature adult was I willing to begin to trust again. For the first time I was able to remember some of these experiences and accept their impact on my life.

One of the most telling images was of a one- or two-year-old lying in a small bed in a strange place, tucked in tight. I had the idea that if I could lie in the bed quiet enough, if I didn't move a muscle all night, I would still be there in the morning. As a child, later, when the family was reunited, I would still try to find a tight, dark place in my bed to create safety and the feeling of being held.

I was trying to figure out the rules for survival. There was some connection between the hurt, the fact that I was rarely held or touched, and the frequent abandonment. I was so young and I needed to understand so much to know what was expected of me. I wanted to know how to protect myself.

Your questions may not be so inwardly turned. You may have community, family, or work issues that you want to know more about. You may seek direction during a time of ambivalence. Sometimes what you receive fits your need but often it can uncover another, deeper need. Whatever happens, you get to decide what to do next.

CHAPTER XVII

TRANSLATING

Profound joy of the heart is like a magnet that indicates the path of life. One has to follow it, even though one enters into a way full of difficulties.

—Mother Teresa

How can we tell the difference between what others do to us and what we do to ourselves?

If it's somebody else, we can stay away from him or her. If it's our own self-image or perception that is the source of confusion or pain, we need to know.

Try evaluating a conflict from both points of view. Put yourself on the other side and argue or try to understand from that position.

If you're hurt, angry, ambivalent, tense, depressed, or afraid, it's probably an inside job.

With most things in life, what is good eventually will feel good, but what merely feels good eventually feels bad.

—Marilyn vos Savant

Being able to tell good from bad in our lives is often difficult. Old patterns will lead us to choose a relationship that is "bad" because it feels "good," or familiar.

Stop to evaluate good and bad in an absolute sense. You know that alcohol abuse, violence, and someone you cannot trust are bad. Self-discipline requires us to choose good over bad regardless of our momentary emotional bent.

When you think the greater good is giving yourself over to something negative, it is far more loving and intelligent to give yourself to something positive.

When your emotions are in conflict with your mind's ability to protect you, choose mind over heart.

You may walk through the door of your shame and find it isn't yours.

—Anonymous

Oh, It's Hell to Get Old!

by Diana Gard Stice*

My mother often used to say, "Oh, it's hell to get old!" She was fifty when I recall her saying this the most, and since to me she looked pretty and healthy, I seriously doubted her. Now that I'm well beyond fifty and could be accurately classified as "old," I understand why my mother said it. She was a diabetic, a divorcee, and feared a bleak future that eventually came to pass.

Despite her negative feelings about herself she encouraged me to develop my musical talent, try to get a college education, and be trained for a career I'd enjoy. She cared about me and I knew it. My father was able to help me pay for my higher education, thus enabling me to get a good job right out of college. I knew he loved me, too.

I had a wonderful time in my first career in education. I received little money for my efforts but had tremendous feelings of success.

After marriage and the birth of a son I trained for another career in education, which I found to be as rewarding as the first one. Marriage and child-rearing were also sources of great joy to me.

---

*Diana Gard Stice is a graduate of San Francisco State University in music and education and holds an M.A. from San Jose State University. She sang with a dance band through college and volunteered at the Stage Door Canteen.

Diana taught high school music for ten years and was a high-school counselor for twenty-eight years. She is now retired. She has participated in choral music productions all her life.

Diana loves to sing, listen to men's choruses, do cross-stitch, read, and be with friends. She has been married for forty years. She has a fine son, a lovely daughter-in-law, and two darling granddaughters.

When retirement time came I felt I could handle anything well, so in the same month I left a job I loved and moved a thousand miles away to a new house in a new state. It was then that I realized that I wasn't coping well with the shock of my actions.

I got sick often. I cried and cried. I made friends, participated in community activities, and still cried a lot. A brief course of medicine for depression just upset my system and didn't help. My husband, always loving and supportive, worried about me. I prayed fervently and often to be guided out of my misery.

I found out that all my tears were caused by grieving for the past—my career, and leaving my dearest friends and familiar place of living. Now it was time to leave grieving and become part of the action again.

I decided to attend a workshop, "Creating Your Future." I realized I did not need to go back to what was comfortable and successful but that I could go ahead to something different.

I became active in my new church, resumed my musical participation, found a marvelous volunteer job, paid visits to my old friends and places whenever I could, traveled a little, and became happy again. I decided that, after all, getting old didn't necessarily need to be hell.

To keep me upbeat I have made a list of things to think about. Here are some of them:

- Happiness requires action.

- Give of your knowledge and experience to help someone.

- Tell your loved ones often how much you love and appreciate them.

- Keep up with what's going on in the world.

- Pay attention to your appearance.

- Become knowledgeable about politics (facts, not hype).

- Get out of the house daily.

- Exercise and eat right (but you may have a hot fudge sundae or a steak sometimes!).

- Have a physical checkup yearly and follow your doctor's advice.

- Notice something good a young person does and mention it to her or him.

- Try to be kind, gracious, and smiling (even if you are filing a complaint).

- Learn a new skill.

- Get a part-time job (employers really want you!).

- Move to a place that's smaller and safer, and dispose of lots of your old stuff (your kids usually don't want it!).

- Write up your memories (your kids will want that).

- Finish your degree.

- Take your grandchildren to sports/musical events.

- Read more.

- Each morning be thankful for another day, another chance; each evening count all your blessings, even the tiniest ones, and give thanks.

- Never give up.

Vision Step Seventeen:
Translating

Once the information is yours, a new barrier is encountered. We resist using what we know to be true. We resist change even when our conscious mind knows it will be positive. We resist even when it is written down. The unconscious resists giving up long-held patterns. The process of translating what we have received can be the longest step in a vision journey.

Joseph Campbell said, "Where your pain is, there is your life." Change always produces a sense of loss, and the grief can be overwhelming. All of the wisdom traditions refer to this abyss, the bottomless pain. You must lean into the pain because the darkest moment holds the truth. The most unprotected time in our night, the hour before dawn, is called the "hour of the wolf" in many cultures.

Out of the darkness always comes the light. Creating alignment among your resources, energies, and visions requires conscious effort. It is a choice you make. My friend Max learned about his life by foreseeing his death. This is his account:

> Imagine yourself in the place I was nearly two years ago. The setting was the Mount Madonna Retreat Center, outside of Santa Cruz. During the quiet of an afternoon's rest in my room a strong inner voice jolted me out of my tranquil state. "Max, you have four years. What is the one thing you will do to have the greatest impact?" Without a moment's hesitation, I heard myself responding, "To create as much magic as I possibly can."
>
> I was shocked and confused. The reference to four years. What did that mean? The end of life? A

new beginning? What do I know about magic, much less creating it?

A lot of thought has since gone into the message of that inner voice. I gathered information on magic. I reflected on what I had read and heard. I listened to that assured laserlike voice inside me. A kaleidoscope of thoughts flashed through my mind. Magic as life's splendid torch. Passion as a hunger deep in the cells of the body. What was the magic?

As a management consultant I had helped organizations examine what they want to look like, feel like, and create for their futures. Organization leaders rarely demonstrated an inclination to embody the ideals and values implied in this type of strategic planning. They were not interested in the "big picture."

I realized it was up to me to design a vision planning procedure that would empower them. I had to help them to know that people can create what they really want. I designed a vision planning program for businesses that would provide inspiration and energy. I knew what my contribution could be.

Max changed his life and his business. He became more successful at both. He could not change the destiny (of a terminal illness that was diagnosed on his return) that had been revealed to him on his retreat, only use it well.

The translating process allows the answers you feel to evolve into a clear image of action. What do you want to do now that you have a handle on the problem or an answer to the question?

I decided I needed to learn how to trust and how to love. I had been an expert but not in my own world. I sought counseling to provide a guide. We joked that I was truly learning the ABC's of love. I had always gone on form before; now I would let myself trust and feel the actual content of a relationship.

The counselor taught me to notice how I was treated and how others responded to the way I treated them. I learned about behavior, not words. I sought out friends who told the truth and were able to touch and be touched. I stayed away from people who had not come to terms with their own monsters.

I finally knew what my assignment was. I became able to transcend my perceived abandonment. I learned to face the conflict in relationships instead of hiding from it. It was hard. My life changed. I am now able to love and be loved. I am no longer tucked tightly in. I am being held. The feeling of abandonment is gone.

CHAPTER XVIII

CHECKING THE FIT

Fortunately analysis is not the only way to resolve inner conflicts. Life itself still remains a very effective therapist.

—Karen Horney

One of life's most fulfilling moments occurs in that split second when the familiar is suddenly transformed into the dazzling aura of the profoundly new.... These breakthroughs are too infrequent, more uncommon than common; and we are mired most of the time in the mundane and the trivial. The shocker: What seems mundane and trivial is the very stuff that discovery is made of. The only difference is our perspective, our readiness to put the pieces together in an entirely new way and to see patterns where only shadows appeared just a moment before.

—Edward B. Lindaman,
Thinking in Future Tense

We all make deals because few situations in life allow for a pure choice. We compromise publicly for the common good and personally because we accept our own limits and therefore the limits of others.

We make deals for work, companionship, sex, love, and family. Learning to do it well, with integrity, is an art. It requires knowing what your values and priorities are. There is always a temptation to be rigid, to be right, at great cost to ourselves and others.

Compromise is something we grow up to. It's a choice to be an adult, to see things the way they are instead of the way we want them to be. It requires that we see others as whole individuals and not as a reflection of ourselves.

Making deals, contracts, and commitments is an internal act, it is an ability to direct our lives, to be responsible for ourselves and for the world we live in. There is often not a right way or a right person. There is only the courage to tell the truth and the willingness to receive the truth.

The world keeps changing at what seems the speed of light. There are so many problems!

The American personality is not working for us as well as it once did. The personality we have inherited may not fit the world we live in.

We may need some adjustments in character to match the changed circumstances we face at home and in the world. We are confronted with powerful shifts in age, ethnicity, resources, environment, technology, politics, markets, and management.

Consider the personality of the future. What kind of future do you want? What kind of person can make it happen? What kind of culture can make it happen? How comfortable would you be with changed responses, defenses, expectations, and motivations?

Here are some personality traits I think are important:*

- When you walk into a room, the safety level of those present increases.

- Your mind has respect for scientific inquiry but is open to intuitive, psychic awareness.

- You would accept an invitation from an extraterrestrial to go up in her spaceship. You believe you are not alone in the universe.

- You are an international citizen. You travel the world in books or in reality. It is easy for you to break bread with people from different racial, ethnic, religious, and national groups.

- You avoid physical violence in any form: guns, corporal punishment, capital punishment, boxing, pit bulls, wrestling. Man's inhumanity to man no longer fascinates you.

---

* Some of the first thoughts for the ideas presented here came from *The Relaxation and Stress Reduction Workbook*, by Martha Davis and others.

- Killing is unacceptable to you. Yet you accept the need to restrain those without conscience. You recognize the presence of madness.

- A sense of humor is one of your most important tools for handling the absurdity that life presents.

- You don't know exactly what you are moving toward. The nature of the goal is open, undefined. You are comfortable with the unknown.

- You are not revolutionary, but evolutionary. You do not want to tear down the system but work slightly beyond it and within it with as much grace as possible.

- You have a long history of aloneness. Yet you have a deep commitment to staying in touch with others. You have many teachers.

- You believe deeply in physical and mental health and do your best to change old, destructive patterns and create new ones.

- If the option of a longer life span were available, you would take it. Yet you have no fear of time.

- You have a passion for life. Your sensuality level is high, but sexuality is not a primary goal.

- You see humanity, in all its forms, as equal. You accept yourself as well as others.

- Reverence for life is a cornerstone of your belief system; all living things qualify for respect.

- Church membership is valuable to you, but you do not feel limited to one form of religion. You believe in the power of the Spirit.

- You are self-disciplined. You are spontaneous but ethical. You will put yourself into unknown places at the expense of security.

153

- You believe in the collective wisdom of society and the truth within yourself. Your primary reward is internal: the pleasure of loving, connecting to the world, and deepening your creativity.

This is only a beginning. Which of these traits apply to you? Which do you think might be essential for the future? How can we teach, encourage, and pass on to our children the characteristics we need for our world?

Vision Step Eighteen:
Checking the Fit

Once the personal vision of the heart begins to surface, it needs to be checked against what we know about ourselves. Do our values, interests, talents, resources, and obligations support what we imagine we want? Does the actual activity of our old life move in the same direction as our vision, or counter to it? How are you directing your energy?

It does not help to know, with an intuitive glow, that you will be happy with less stuff to move around if at that moment you are ordering more stuff from a catalog. Habits of reassurance are hard to break and hard to replace with new habits of internal safety. The more powerful and personal your vision, the more it demands of you.

This is a time when it helps to lay out a treasure map. Put the dream or goal at one end of a road and you at the other. Try to imagine the barriers that are in your way, or record them as they occur. Awareness is everything. A visual diary of the pitfalls in your personality helps. Most of us carry old convictions that disallow satisfaction or prevent risk.

Visions are meant to enhance your life and the life of your community. They are not meant to turn it upside down. Your vision is not considered to be true in any wisdom tradition if it is not for the good of the community. It must have meaning beyond your own ego needs. How does what you know fit with the life you are living? Can you follow it and still meet your responsibilities and the laws of your culture?

If you need more freedom to be creative, it does not mean that you can abandon your children or commitments. Checking the fit means literally seeing how you can hold on to your visions, change your life, and still follow your basic moral code. If you need to leave people there will be questions of how to participate in a gentle and ethical process of change.

You will probably have to take some risks as you make changes. You will confront some people in your life when you try to clear out the past. You will look at your house, work, community, service, politics, and religion in different ways. You will start thinking about groups or individuals who would offer support for the changes you want to make.

People with a sense of personal vision truly believe they have the power to create their own reality or that the right reality has been revealed to them. They are willing to ask themselves over and over again: "What do I really want? What has heart for me?" They follow their visions. They exercise personal power through conscious choice.

CHAPTER XIX

MAKING THE COMMITMENT

Until one is committed, there is hesitancy, the chance to draw back, always ineffectiveness, concerning all acts of initiative and creation. The moment one definitely commits oneself, then Providence moves, too.

—J. W. von Goethe

Since Martin's death in Memphis and that tremen-
dous day in Atlanta, something has altered in me,
something has gone away. Perhaps even more than
the death itself, the manner of his death has forced
me into a judgment concerning human life and
human beings which I have always been reluctant to
make....Incontestably, alas most people are not, in
action, worth very much; and yet every human being
is an unprecedented miracle. One tries to treat them
as the miracles they are, while trying to protect one-
self against the disasters they've become.

— James Baldwin,
in *James Baldwin: Artist on Fire,*
by W. J. Weatherby

There are transitions in our lives always—often when we least expect them—times when we choose or are forced into a deep shift in our lives and being; death, psychic change, separation, loss of work, disability.

These are times of growth, a stretching of all we are and can be. You know about the resistance and the pain. Remind yourself of the reward. The joy is always equal to the suffering.

What we forget and struggle with is the neutral zone between. It is a time of quiet. We miss the intensity. Be patient, let go of the struggle, breathe deeply. You are not lost, not even marking time. You need the rest. Trust, let the transition unfold. Nature is on your side.

This is a time of healing, of moving the new quality within you into bedrock.

As the wind and rain of Seattle force me inside, the sun is replaced in part by dreams: new work, books to read, projects to build, places to go, and friends to love. Listening to the heart within.

Joseph Campbell calls it "following your bliss."

Carlos Castaneda describes it as "the path with heart."

Langston Hughes wrote, "A dream deferred dries up like a raisin in the sun."

Dreams never go away. They haunt us as shadows of the part of our life never lived. Few regret pursuing a dream if it doesn't work out. Most of us regret not trying.

When it comes to dreams, decisions of the head over the heart are the ones we may regret most deeply. Whatever the opposition—practical, time, relatives, fear, or lack of faith—a dream deferred too long is a bit of life lost.

Respect your dreams.

Vision Step Nineteen:
Making the Commitment

Once the answers are yours, the next step is whether you wish to act on them. Try to formulate some plans or at least a step in the direction you wish to go while you are still alone. You will be withdrawing now from the vulnerability of your experience, so you may feel ambivalent about how to put your knowledge directly into your life.

Review the schedule you carry each week, review the things you do, review the wedges of your life again, and write down at least one change you are willing to commit to. In my case it was obvious: Take steps to reduce the possibility of further abandonment, and strengthen my belief that I could create safety for myself. That meant giving up a relationship I had been struggling with and choosing new friends with greater care.

The vision process puts you in a vulnerable state because you have laid aside some of your routine defenses. We learn many techniques to keep our deepest thoughts at bay, busyness being the most common. When you slow yourself down and open up, it takes a while to restore your defenses and filters.

When you decide to return home, if you have taken a physical as well as spiritual journey, keep this in mind. Try to reenter your work and activities at a slow pace. You will be preoccupied, vague, ambivalent. Note how you feel, and don't push yourself. We should ease both into and out of journeys. You may feel you are in neutral, but changes are taking place within. Try to avoid situations or people who will draw energy away from you.

Keep your vision experiences to yourself until they have become a more stable part of your being. Others will sense the change in you, the increased power, and it will make some peo-ple uncomfortable. Spend your time with people who offer sup-port and acceptance.

When you find yourself around people threatened by the change, be prepared for negative responses. If you share infor-mation, they may try to sabotage you and reduce your power to a level they are comfortable with. Even the most loving of your friends may resist your changes because it will ultimately affect or reflect on them.

Give yourself time to check the fit, again, of the informa-tion you have received before announcing specific changes or involving others. Review your plans and your commitment.

Remember that you must be responsible to those whose lives are directly affected by your choices. They must be treat-ed in a sensitive and ethical manner. Let them participate in any process that affects them. Decide how you can hold on to your new goal if others disagree or are threatened.

Use your mind as well as your emotions to lay your plans. Small steps toward your goal are much more likely to be suc-cessful than large ones. If you want to exercise to feel healthier, commit to a small step that will take you in that direction. It may be too hard actually to go to the pool, but you could hang your swimsuit on the front doorknob.

There are many ways to change. Here are the common styles; the example is food. Check what you have been doing since returning home and see which one seems to fit you.

Substitution: You decide to quit smoking but you substitute food and gain weight.

Incremental: You give up one food that you have decided is bad for you, but you keep all the rest. This change is like adding a new little bump to your being but does not involve a major system shift.

Pendulum: You become a macrobiotic vegetarian and devote large amounts of your time to processing and discussing food. You may try to convert others to your way of thinking because it has become a dominant force in your life. You may have gone from one closed way of thinking to another.

None of these change styles will give you what a vision can offer. Incremental change has value, but the others may leave you, in a few months, back where you started. Transformation of the whole system, a deep and permanent change, is the gift of a successful vision journey.

You take care of your health in every way, not in inconsistent bits or through a rigid system. You change your eating habits, but it is neither a diet nor a rigid philosophy. It is a comfort within your body and what you know to be good for you. Something within you relaxes.

The transformation style of change is called a "paradigm shift." Your entire way of thought about the issue is altered. People who do take their visions seriously become the achievers and leaders who create change in ways that were once thought impossible.

CHAPTER XX

TRANSFORMATION

Every breath taken by the man who loves and the woman who loves goes to fill the water tank where the spirit horses drink.

—Robert Bly

Some signs and symptoms of inner peace:

- A tendency to think and act spontaneously rather than from fear based on past experiences.
- An unmistakable ability to enjoy each moment.
- Loss of interest in judging other people.
- Loss of interest in judging self.
- Loss of interest in interpreting the actions of others.
- Loss of interest in conflict.
- Loss of ability to worry.
- Frequent, overwhelming episodes of appreciation.
- Content feelings of connection with others and nature.
- An increasing tendency to let things happen rather than to make them happen.
- An increased susceptibility to love extended by others, as well as the uncontrollable urge to extend it.

After a time of decay comes the turning point. The powerful light that has been banished returns. There is movement, but it is not brought about by force....The movement is natural, arising spontaneously. For this reason the transformation of the old becomes easy. The old is discarded and the new is introduced. Both measures accord with time; therefore no harm results.

—I Ching

I used to lie in my bed at Girl Scout camp on Lake Coeur d'Alene and figure that I'd know what was going on by the time I was twenty-one.

Certainly, I thought when I was twenty-one that I'd have life understood by twenty-five. That was old; I'd be a fool not to know by then.

At thirty I said, "So this is it. Well, I think I understand." At thirty-three I kept singing, painfully, the lines from the song "What's It All About, Alfie?" I felt settled at thirty-five; this must be it. But I found myself revising all I knew at thirty-nine.

Now I'm forty. Almost halfway physically, just starting philosophically and spiritually. At peace personally, until next week changes me. Just starting to figure it all out.

Maybe by forty-five.

Next week I will be fifty. Wow! Some parts of me still feel seventeen. Am I only moments away from those days when I was ten, at Lake Coeur d'Alene?

I'm sure I know when I'll understand it all. It will be at that moment, well into my nineties, when I draw the last breaths and say to myself, "Oh, that was it."

It is odd to age. Not painful because there are rewards and trade-offs. But there is also loss. Ours is a culture that celebrates youth and beauty, particularly in women, and it is unlikely to change anytime soon.

Having laid out that truth, I can counter it by reminding you and me of the incredible pleasures that come with the deepening of self that is part of long life experience: self-knowledge, stronger values, awareness of one's competence, independence, freedom from competition, an identity separate from men and family, kinship with the world, and more reasonable expectations are all wonders that come with getting older.

Research on happiness indicates that if health remains good, women report their happiest years are their sixties and seventies. There are many reasons cited, but the ones that stand out in the surveys are that there are fewer people to please and no one is left to push them around anymore. Some women reach sixty before they feel they can truly run their own life. It will probably be easier for our generation because we started running more of our own lives sooner.

The key to getting older with pleasure is just that—running your own life. If we continue to live by others' expectations, we will age by them, too. Fortunately, we are creating our own.

I am lucky: I have some great role models for aging. My mother at seventy-seven swims every day, travels the world, is closely involved in her community through church and politics, and is very happily married. She and her husband of ten years sat holding hands the last time I visited and, with tears in their eyes, told me how surprised they were to have encountered so much love so late in their lives.

I have some friends in their seventies and eighties whose lives are clearly wonderful. I just bought a house from a dynamic, creative woman of eighty-seven. She had, as a teacher, lived and was living a full life. The house was filled with light, color, plants, and classical music. Her spirit was in the walls and the garden, a wonderful inheritance.

Her expectations of life had been met because she is of a generation that had expectations more rooted in reality than my own. True, there were fantasies that may not have come true, but not desires for wealth, romance, and experience that could not be met.

I believe we have created expectations that cannot be met in reality. Whether it is career fulfillment, housekeeping, parenting or romance, we wonder if we are becoming jaded instead of realizing that our eyes are opening. There is more to be enjoyed with full awareness, but the frilly edges are gone.

When the Valentine's Day commercial bash is in full swing, I spend only a second wondering about roses because I have begun to accept romance as it really is and not as it is sold. The most loving people in the world often cannot talk about love or make stereotypical gestures because they feel too deeply.

We expect so much of ourselves as parents, but no one has a perfect childhood. I used to see families through their picture windows as I delivered the papers on my paper route and think that they were "real" American families. My life would be different if I had one of those. If my mother baked cookies and did the laundry, I would have had an easier life. How absurd, I now realize. It's always a mixed bag for parents and children. We should work as hard as we can to be loving and thoughtful parents, but we will never be all things to anyone.

Housekeeping is the easy example of the absurdities of our expectations about life. If you live in an immaculate house, I assume you are not a happy person. It requires far too much control to clean in detail, consistently. Passion is messy, and so is life. Happy older people begin to understand the balance between order and passion and opt to play more and worry about the grout in the shower less.

We grow up thinking we can be everything to everyone. Within each of us are so many men and women to be. We want all that tradition has told us to be and all the new possibilities we can envision and feel. Taking responsibility for our own lives requires us to choose what we will give and take. Each transition, each birthday, or anniversary is a time to review these choices.

Remember where you have been and decide where you want to go. When you create a positive image of yourself five or ten years in the future, it becomes a time filled with possibilities instead of losses.

I want to feel strong and at peace. The decisions I make now about values, my place in the world, my relationships and financial security will determine my options in the future.

I know I must stay physically fit, invest in my friendships and support systems, take full responsibility for my financial security, protect my personal safety, stay involved in my community, prepare for the unexpected, and remember to enjoy myself. I know I'll keep my sense of humor and perspective. My friends and I all plan to be eccentrics.

If this is a halfway mark, it feels good. I can sit in bed and see the ferry crossing Puget Sound. I like my husband, my friends, my child, my mother, my work, my neighborhood, and my dog.

I like all the things I feel coming up ahead: learning more about love, becoming better at my work. Anthropologists do their best thinking in their fifties. Maybe there will be a grandchild, less greed and more compassion in the world, a puppy, and the chance to create a new garden.

I've moved a lot in the past few years. Now I've settled into a new house we have built. It is on the opposite side of Seattle from our old house. We have exchanged the sunrise view in our old home above a lake for the sunset of the sound. It feels good; Lake Washington was limited but Puget Sound goes on forever. The newer wrinkles and puckers in my face are softer in this light, in this place.

Vision Step Twenty:
Transformation

The last step of a vision journey is a paradigm shift. The information you receive on your journey is so powerful, it creates a new perspective that alters every part of your life. There is a moment of synthesis and integration where your values become clear.

> *The genius of this kind of leadership lies in the transcending ability, a kind of magic, to assemble, out of all the variety of images, signals, forecasts and alternatives, a clearly articulated vision of the future that is at once simple, easily understood, clearly desirable and energizing.*

—Warren Bennis

I have made this transformation in the areas of my life I have given over to the vision experience. Now, whenever I feel afraid or limited, I can push through the barrier to the other side. I can lean into the pain instead of away from it. I can move through it. Knowing and coming to terms with the handle of my shadow, "abandonment," have given me strength, understanding, forgiveness, and acceptance. I feel and think at a deeper level now, more of a realist, more in tune, happier, able to cruise instead of run and making better choices of who I give my heart to. I sense there is some wonderful work in my future. I am wiser.

A paradigm shift does not lead to perfection. There will always be changes and missteps. It does create a clarity about what you want and your commitment to it.

How much a part of your daily life and thought has the information you received on your journey become? Has it changed the way you treat yourself? Has it changed the way you treat others? Something as simple as noticing when your stomach is full or when you are most likely to eat in a way you don't want to indicates a changed thought pattern.

I've used health as an example and my own fears, but these ideas apply to all life processes. If you have a vision of your connections to others, it will change the way you treat them. You will have moments of feeling like a citizen of the world. If your change is in personal relationships, you will become more aware of how people respond to you instead of being detached. When you ask your friend for something, you will notice if he is able to give it to you.

Transformation is the process of achieving your vision. Embodiment is the feeling of it becoming an integral part of you. They add up to a successful vision experience. Transformation is the completion of a vision, the moment when you are what you wanted to be. Your life reflects the commitment you made.

Here is just one more example of this process in my own life.

Years ago I imagined two people talking about me around the corner at the medical school where I was teaching. What did I want to overhear them saying? I cared so much about what others thought of me. I imagined they would say, "She's smart, she'll be a full professor," etc. Instead, what I heard in my imagination is, "She cares." It changed my life. I began to be much more involved in my community and eventually left the university.

One evening five years later I was introduced as a speaker at a banquet. The person introducing me went through the usual list of credits and ended by gesturing toward me and saying, "She is a woman who cares." I began to cry because what I was and what I wanted to be were becoming one. It was one of the supreme moments of my life.

When I faced a painful divorce some years later I repeated the exercise. This time I heard them saying, "She's decent." I thought that was pretty useless until I realized that perhaps all I could hold on to in this sad time were my ethics. I realized that long after I had healed from the loss of love I would have to face how I had behaved. The knowledge lifted my depression.

I asked the question again, two years later, when I had

recovered from the divorce. The disembodied voices around the corner said with a chuckle, "She's still trying to figure it out." They were right, and that was okay.

The last time I used this exercise I received the most powerful of responses. The voices said, gently, "She has learned to love."

As I complete this page I go through the exercise again and the voices startle me. "She doesn't care." What does that mean? I'm still a caring person. Then I understand how true the statement is. I don't need to know what others think of me anymore. The question has lost its meaning.

The vision process is a way to stay in touch with yourself and the higher resources of the world you live in. You are always changing, so your main assignment is always to know in what direction you are going. This journey is a lifetime one because a completed vision releases energy for a revision or the opening to a new vision.

> *If you follow your bliss, you put yourself on a kind of track that has been there all the while, waiting for you, and the life you ought to be living is the one you are living. Wherever you are—if you are following your bliss, you are enjoying that refreshment, that life within you, all the time."*

> —Joseph Campbell,
> *The Power of Myth*

It is a heroic act to make even the smallest change that contributes to the life of this world. Someday I hope someone will introduce me to a group with the words, "She is a woman who has learned to love."

There is no vision more powerful than one that links you to all of life. There is no love that rewards more consistently than the love one has for the world. Slow down, breathe deeply, let go, follow your heart, and the universe will move.

ACKNOWLEDGMENTS

All copyrighted quotes were reprinted with the permission of the publisher, as listed below.

p. 1   From *The Power of Myth* © 1988 by Joseph Campbell. Reprinted by permission of Doubleday, a division of Bantam Doubleday Dell Publishing Group, Inc.

p. 5   From *The Pregnant Virgin* © 1985 by Marion Woodman. Reprinted by permission of Inner City Books.

p. 6   From *The Finishing School* by Gail Godwin. Copyright © 1984 by Gail Godwin. Used by permission of Viking Penguin, a division of Penguin Books USA, Inc.

p. 17   From *Brief Lives* © 1991 by Anita Brookner. Reprinted by permission of Random House, Inc.

p. 25   From *The Temper of Our Times* © 1967 by Eric Hoffer. Reprinted by permission of HarperCollins Publishers.

p. 27   From *The Course in Miracles: A Gift for All Mankind* © 1990 by Tara Singh. Reprinted by permission of Life Action Press.

p. 29   From *The Power of Myth* © 1988 by Joseph Campbell. Reprinted by permission of Doubleday, a division of Bantam Doubleday Dell Publishing Group, Inc.

p. 33   From *For Your Own Good* © 1983 by Alice Miller. Reprinted by permission of Farrar, Straus & Giroux, Inc.

p. 47   From "East Coker," in *Four Quartets* by T.S. Eliot. Copyright 1943 by T.S. Eliot; renewed 1971 by Esme Valerie Eliot. Reprinted by permission of Harcourt Brace Jovanovich, Inc.

p. 49   From *The Power of Myth* © 1988 by Joseph Campbell. Reprinted by permission of Doubleday, a division of Bantam Doubleday Dell Publishing Group, Inc.

p. 53   From *Emmanuel's Book* © 1985 by Pat Rodegast and Judith Stanton. Reprinted by permission of Bantam Books, a division of Bantam Doubleday Dell Publishing Group, Inc.

p. 54   From *The Journey* © 1954 by Lillian Smith. Reprinted by permission of Norton.

p. 58   Excerpt from *The Passionate Life* by Sam Keen. Copyright © 1983 by Sam Keen. Reprinted by permission of HarperCollins Publishers.

ABOUT THE AUTHOR

Jennifer James, Ph.D., one of the country's most popular lecturers and the author of seven books including the best-selling *Success Is the Quality of Your Journey* and *Windows*, holds a doctorate in cultural anthropology and master's degrees in both history and psychology. For almost twelve years, she has written a weekly column for the *Seattle Times* and, as one of the area's most popular commentators, hosted a daily talk shows that helped people understand psychology, culture, perception, and the choices they are making in their lives. She lectures worldwide to school, university, and profesional groups, including ITT, IBM, Boeing, and the Young Presidents' Organization. Dr. James lives in Seattle, Washington.

Jennifer James has helped thousands to change their attitudes from the conventional yardstick of success—and to lead happier, more peace-filled lives. Reward a friend with Dr. James's writings on how to stop the grind and share the moments of pleasure and warmth.

Visions: Tapping into spiritual teachings and mythologies, James takes her readers on a step-by-step journey to self-discovery and personal change. Illustrated. Trade paperback. 192 pages.

Success Is the Quality of Your Journey: 120 insights and ideas on subjects such as risk, solitude, aging, and relationships. Trade paperback. 144 pages.

Windows: 120 more essays on the topics of day-to-day living, intimacy, heroic acts, traveling (including the author's journey to Nepal), and more. Trade paperback. 160 pages.

You Know I Wouldn't Say This If I Didn't Love You: How to Defend Yourself Against Verbal Zaps and Zingers: Filled with nitty-gritty advice for both the giver and getter of criticism, James's book will help readers defend themselves from—and laugh at—the absurd and harmful things we say to each other. Illustrated. Trade paperback. 144 pages.

Ask for these titles at your local bookstore, or order by mail today.

Use this coupon, or write to:
Newmarket Press, 18 East 48th Street, New York, NY 10017
212-832-3575

Please send me:

_____ copies of *Visions,* @ $9.95 each;

_____ copies of *Success,* @ $9.95 each;

_____ copies of *Windows,* @ $9.95 each;

_____ copies of *You Know I Wouldn't Say This If I Didn't Love You,* @ $10.95 each.

Please include applicable sales tax, and add $2.00 for postage and handling (plus $1.00 for each additional item ordered)—check or money order only. Please allow 4-6 weeks for delivery. Prices and availability are subject to change.

Enclosed is a check or money order, payable to Newmarket Press, in the amount of $ _____

Name _____

Address _____

City/State/Zip _____

Companies, professional groups, clubs, and other organizations may qualify for special terms on quantity purchases of these titles. For more information, please phone or write: Special Sales Department, Newmarket Press, 18 East 48th Street, New York, N.Y. 10017 (212) 832-3575.